Helen,
Happy networking &
best wishes.. ☺

THE FROG AND PRINCE

THE FROG AND PRINCE

Secrets of Positive Networking™ ...to change your life

by **Darcy Rezac**
with Judy Thomson and Gayle Hallgren

foreword by **Tom Donohue**
President and CEO, U.S. Chamber of Commerce

Frog and Prince Networking Corporation
www.frogandprince.com

Canadian Cataloguing in Publication Data

Rezac, Darcy, 1946-
The frog and prince : secrets of positive networking to change your life / by Darcy Rezac with Judy Thomson and Gayle Hallgren.

Includes bibliographical references.
ISBN 0-9732265-0-1

1. Business networks. 2. Success in business. I. Thomson, Judy, 1954- II. Hallgren, Gayle, 1951- III. Title.
HD69.S8R49 2003 650.1'3 C2002-911531-0

Jacket and text design: Jacqueline Verkley
Illustration: Kathy Boake
Editing: Pam Withers (www.pamwithers.com)
Author photos: Dave Roels
Printed and bound in Canada by Friesens

First printing: February 2003
Second printing: May 2003
Third printing: January 2005

CONTENTS

FOREWORD		VII
PREFACE		XI
THE ORIGINAL TALE		XV
CHAPTER 1	Frogs, Princes & Toads	1
CHAPTER 2	Networking—The Power Defined	11
CHAPTER 3	**N**: Never Leave Home Without Them	29
CHAPTER 4	**E**: The Four E's—Establish, Extend, Exchange, Engage	47
CHAPTER 5	**T**: Travel In Pairs	69
CHAPTER 6	**W**: Working The Pond—Positively	81
CHAPTER 7	**O**: Opportunity Is Everywhere	105
CHAPTER 8	**R**: Repeat, Repeat, Repeat	131
CHAPTER 9	**K**: Keep It Going	145
CHAPTER 10	Happily Ever After	165
AFTERWORD		175
ACKNOWLEDGMENTS		179
APPENDIX I	Tips For Good Business Card Design	183
BIBLIOGRAPHY		187
VISIT OUR POND		189

FOREWORD

by Thomas J. Donohue
President and CEO, U.S. Chamber of Commerce

Watch out successful networkers—your best-kept secrets are now out of the bag!

You have Darcy Rezac to thank for this. In *The Frog and Prince: Secrets of Positive Networking*, Darcy opens up the world of networking and lays it out for all to see—in an understandable, entertaining and compelling way.

Have you talked yourself into believing that you're not cut out to be a successful networker? This book will give you the confidence to succeed.

Are you one who just doesn't like to network? This book shows you how it can be fun and rewarding.

Do you believe that personal networking is outmoded and unnecessary in a transparent world of process, procedure and technology? This book will shake you out of that mistaken belief.

Think you're already a pretty good networker and there's nothing you can learn from any book? You'll be pleasantly surprised starting with the very first chapter.

Let me be honest. I think I'm a pretty good networker. I credit much of the success I have enjoyed to the circle of friends, colleagues, associates and contacts I've developed around the world in all walks of life over more years than I care to remember. Yet I have found plenty of fresh insights in this book.

Darcy is just the one to set it all out for us. From his high positions in government and business, to his training in psychology and travels all over the world, Darcy has the background and range of experience to peel off the layers of mystery and misunderstanding that have obscured successful networking for too long. And by studying, writing and lecturing on the topic for more than two decades, he knows how to reach his audience, to make the complex seem simple, and to make the painstaking follow-up and follow-through of networking actually seem enjoyable.

While Darcy draws on an age-old fairy tale for inspiration, his lessons could not be more timely. In a world full of change and uncertainty, the reach and durability of your personal network are more important than ever. Careers are changing, businesses are merging and companies are restructuring. The world is shrinking and opening up but growing more complex. Believe me, time and time again you will find yourself calling upon—and sometimes leaning on—your network to get yourself back on track or to unearth exciting new opportunities. And your network will expect the same of you.

But more important than all of this is the compelling link Darcy establishes between successful positive networking and personal happiness.

I chose that last word carefully. Yes, networking is critical to career success. Yes, it can lead to an improved financial picture. But for me, the most rewarding aspect of networking is the personal happiness it has brought. My own life has been greatly enriched by the hundreds if not thousands of people from all backgrounds I have gotten to know and had an opportunity to help. It has been particularly satisfying to follow their careers and lives over the years, watching them grow and succeed or helping them bounce back from a loss or failure. And it's always been a comfort to have so many people to call upon for help and advice. I have done it many times!

Positive networking can do much more than help you succeed; it can help you become a better, more giving person, a person who makes a real contribution to society and to all those around you.

When all is said and done, that is going to be your legacy on this earth. Not what positions you held or how much money you made, but how you treated other people and how they remember you—from your own family, to those you worked with, to all those with whom you have come into contact. Whenever I speak to students at their commencements or in the classroom, I always make sure to tell them this.

Great rewards can flow from positive networking and only some of them are about money and success. For me the outstanding achievement of *The Frog and Prince* is that Darcy does not just tell us "how"—he tells us "why."

So read, learn, enjoy, act and start reaping the many wonderful benefits that come from positive networking.

Thomas J. Donohue
Washington, D.C.
January 2003

PREFACE

It was a warm summer's evening and John Hunter was patiently waiting in line to see The Phantom of the Opera. The musical had just opened on Broadway. John, a self-admitted "Phantom nut," had flown in from the West Coast just to see it. Over the noise of the traffic, John heard a man behind him speaking Spanish. Many years earlier, John had worked in South America as an engineer for the energy firm Petróleos de Venezuela, and was fluent in Spanish. So he turned and started chatting.

To his amazement, John realized that this man was his Venezuelan manager's boss—someone he hadn't seen in over fifteen years. What were the odds?

Two months later—out of the blue—John was invited by an international engineering firm to be a senior consultant on a large Venezuelan energy project. Guess who had put his name forward? It is indeed a small world.

Networks are powerful things, especially human ones. As it turns out, and as you will discover in this book, John's network story is not all that unusual. Similar stories happen all the time. It's the magic of random and unexpected good things that flow to those who network well, and to those whom they touch. It is what is defined in these pages as *the secrets of positive networking*™.

I have been a student of networking for more than two decades and continue to be surprised at how few *great* networkers there really are. I regularly ask my *Secrets of Positive Networking*™ seminar participants to name the great networkers they know. Few identify more than a handful. It seems that great networkers are not often spotted in the wild, or anywhere else for that matter. Just ask anyone.

Well then, how about *good* networkers? I ask seminar participants how many consider themselves good at the craft. It's usually fewer than ten percent. Then I ask, "How many people here really enjoy networking?" Less than twenty percent put up their hands—eighty percent don't like to do it. This is an astounding number given that networking is such an essential skill for both personal and business success.

If so few like it and even fewer are good at it and the greats are scarce, what does it all mean? It means there's lots of room at the top—it's certainly not crowded—and, as you will discover, it is not all that difficult to get there. Those who understand the power of positive networking know that great networking skills can be learned by anyone. It's like learning to dance. With the knowledge, patience, practice and right attitude, anyone can learn the necessary steps to *the network dance.* And the top slots are not reserved for a privileged few. They are open to all who acquire the skills and use them well.

For a variety of reasons, too many people prefer not to participate in networking. Some are uncomfortable doing it, some just don't think it's time well spent, and some don't think it works. For others, it is a lack of understanding or awareness, or a combination of both. Whatever the reason, there is good news. Networking is worth doing because it is such an important life skill; it works powerfully when it is done well.

Successful leaders and achievers have understood the power of networks since the beginning of time, but this anecdotal evidence has also recently been proven by science. Researchers at Cornell University in the late 1990s, using mathematical graph theory, discovered the astonishing power of the "small-worlds phenomenon." This was groundbreaking proof of what had been folklore—that each of us is connected to everyone else on the planet with just a few handshakes. John Hunter tapped into the power of it all that summer's night in a theatre line-up.

That's the good news. Positive networking works, and it works well. The great news is that those who already network can do it better. Those who don't, can learn the skills of positive networking and become good at it. In fact, any one of us can become a *great networker.*

That's what *The Frog and Prince* is all about. It is learning that we all start out just like the frog in the Grimm brothers' fable, and that we too can become *a prince or princess of networking.*

Darcy Rezac

THE ORIGINAL TALE

Most of us grew up learning the tale of the *Frog Prince*. Actually, the story has its origins in the Grimm Brothers' *The Frog King.* It's the story of a princess whose golden ball falls into a pond. A frog appears and tells her that he will retrieve her ball if she will invite him back to the castle and let him be her companion. She quickly agrees but once the frog gives her the ball, the princess just walks away. Later that evening the pushy frog knocks on the door of the castle demanding the princess fulfill her promise. She is a true princess—in every sense of the word—and doesn't care if she breaks her promise to such a disgusting little creature. Her father, the King, chastises her for not treating the frog nicely and demands that she keep her promise.

Then the story gets a little racy. The frog demands to share her bed as part of the deal. She agrees, but she is a princess with a plan. Picking up the little frog between two fingers she goes to her bedroom and throws him against the wall. Splat. He slides down into her bed transformed into a handsome prince and the rest we will leave to your imagination.

Over the years, this classic story has been changed into different versions of the original tale. The one most of us know is a toned-down modern version where the princess just kisses a frog, the frog turns into a prince and they live happily every after. It's become a common figure of speech: kissing a frog to find a prince.

the beginning

CHAPTER ONE

frogs, princes & toads

Kissing Frogs

Once upon a time, there was an entrepreneurial young chorus frog named Lily, who was invited to a networking event at The Palace—The Palace Hotel, that is. For moral support, she took her older and more experienced brother as her guest.

Lily was looking for a prince or two. Actually, she was looking for good business contacts, but she knew that most of the people at The Palace would probably be "just frogs." Since Lily understood the laws of probability, she also knew she'd have to kiss a lot of frogs to find a prince or two. Actually, she only had to give them her business card, and she was okay with that.

FROGS, PRINCES & TOADS

When I first thought about writing a book on networking, I was reminded of something my wife, Gayle, said to me when we started dating. In those days, I had to schedule my dates with her some time in advance, as her dance card was pretty full. When I commented on this, she quickly replied, "You've got to kiss a lot of frogs to find a prince."

SO WHAT IS A FROG?

Forget the stereotype about frogs—green and slimy. We're all frogs until we find the right match. Yes, it can be a romantic match, but this book is primarily about networking, not dating (although the theory is the same).

In networking, you want to meet enough frogs to become a "frog about the pond," and to turn some of those fellow frogs into business contacts of princely proportions. The good news is that no one has to kiss any frogs. Like Lily, you just give them your business card.

WHO POPULATES THE FROG POND?

Here's a guide to some of the frogs you will meet in this book (and at networking events):

THE FROG CHAIN

THE ROYALS (*Amphibius rex et regina*)

These are the princes and princesses of networking. They are rarely found in the wild, or anywhere else for that matter. Even the best networkers have a hard time naming more than seven royals. We will know one when we spot one.

THE TREE FROGS (Amphibius borealis)

These are unusually good networkers. By reputation they stand tall in the amphibian world and see beyond the bounds of the kingdom. Although they are on the road to royalty, only a few will make it. What they know and who they know sets them apart from the chorus.

THE CHORUS FROGS (Pseudacris musicalis)

These frogs have decided to take the plunge and join the chorus. They actually practice the art of "ribbiting" (engaging contacts) expecting to get results. They achieve varying degrees of success. Some become good networkers. Chorus frogs have decided to get their feet wet.

JUST FROGS (Amphibius normalis)

We are all born frogs. A surprisingly high number decide not to come out of the weeds and participate in the network dance, at least for the time being. They prefer to stay—sorry folks—just frogs.

THE TOADS (Bufo obnoxios)

A few frogs decide to move *down* the frog chain. They are not hard to spot. While mercifully scarce, they are sure to be there to run into.

! WARNING: From the Amphibian Surgeon-General

Do not rush to categorize contacts by the frog chain. Treat everyone like royalty. One person's frog may be another's prince. The chain is best used for self-assessment.

WHOLE LOT OF HANDSHAKIN'

I have spent my career in networking ponds and have met everyone in the frog chain. To calculate my pond time, I have emulated my favorite author, the aviator Ernest K. Gann. Here's a passage from his book, *A Hostage to Fortune*:

> *...How many days have I existed? Answer, if I have the present date correct: 24,455 days and nights, not counting time spent in the fetal stage... I have read a mere 5,460 books... I have tried the patience of my friends while consuming a minimum of 5,160 bottles of wine... To my astonishment I next find that my heart has beat at least two billion times...*

Unlike Ernest Gann, I start counting my networking experience not from birth, but from when I first took my job as the managing director of The Vancouver Board of Trade in 1986. Formed in 1887, The Board is a privately funded business association with more than a century of history as a champion of free enterprise. With more than 450 networking events a year, The Board offers members an incredibly rich and diverse networking environment. While I was networking long before taking this job, it all pales by comparison.

> *...How many networking experiences have I had? Answer: I estimate that I have been introduced to 320,000 people face to face. I have been to over 2,500 receptions, 3,000 speaker breakfasts, luncheons, dinners and innumerable gala events. I have worn out more than my fair share of tuxedos.*

And I've networked in some of the strangest places, from the floor of the New York Stock Exchange at midnight to a circling Lockheed P-3 patrol aircraft at 200 feet above the North Pole.

Add to this another 100 or so outside events per year including conferences and trade missions. Everything from going to a week-long business and world leaders' summit in Davos, Switzerland annually since 1989, to speaking at the Rotary Club in the Yukon. What you've got is a whole lot of handshakin' going on.

As a student of networking, I have been witness to some of the world's best in action. In addition to a plethora of top business leaders—such as American Airlines CEO Don Carty and Dell Computer Corporation's Chairman and CEO Michael Dell—thousands of great networkers and distinguished visitors have spoken at The Board. These have included George Bush Sr., Hong Kong's Anson Chan, Corazon Aquino of the Philippines, Prince Philip, The Body Shop's Anita Roddick, Nobel Prize winner Robert Mundell, Sinn Fein's Gerry Adams and primatologist Jane Goodall, to name only a few. For me, The Board has been an incredible window on the world of networking.

GAYLE AND JUDY

My co-authors Gayle and Judy bring their own perspectives to this book, based on their different networking experiences.

Gayle is a successful entrepreneur and marketing consultant—a very adventurous person both personally and in her business endeavors. With the positive attitude of a good networker, Gayle has attended hundreds of events and been the tablemate of some of the world's most interesting people. She has also sat through fifteen-course meals where each dish was stranger than the last. I have been fortunate to call her my tag-teammate for the past decade, and I have learned a lot from her.

Judy is a chartered accountant, trainer and team builder extraordinaire. For her, the ultimate network is a well-functioning team. She has developed and managed teams in a variety of cultures and environments—from the gleaming office towers of North America, Hong Kong and Beijing to a tiny swaying office at the back of a rail coach. From a job as senior member of an international accounting and consulting firm to one as the jack-of-all-trades customer service director at the startup of one of North America's most successful rail tour companies, she has experienced every nuance of international business networking.

THE END RESULT

What's the end result of all this fieldwork? We have seen The Good, The Bad and the Just Plain Ugly. The Good are the great networkers. It comes naturally to them; it's just what they do. These are the princes and princesses of networking. You want to know them and become one. At the other end of the scale are the Just Plain Ugly. These you want to avoid. Fortunately, they are few and far between.

Sad to say, but The Bad are the majority of us. (Okay, maybe we're not so bad; we're just not great.) In a networking situation, we frogs tend to do a lot of things that lessen our effectiveness. These include:

- not giving out business cards
- setting our expectations too high
- investing a lot of energy in a few select people we already know
- not engaging in conversation
- missing the really great opportunities around us every day
- being unaware we are in a networking situation
- and most importantly: having no joy when we network

THE STEPS AND SECRETS

Great networkers have a natural rhythm; there's nothing forced in how they network. For them, it's an easy habit, and they seem to enjoy themselves. The good news is that it's a skill that can be learned. It involves just seven easy steps. To learn the moves, all you have to do is follow *The Network Dance: N.E.T.W.O.R.K.*™

To make it even simpler, there is a chapter devoted to each step. As with all dance skills, it takes practice and patience to learn how to glide about the pond without stepping on anyone's toes, but it is something you can start tomorrow. If from time to time you need a refresher, just read the summary at the end of each chapter to remind yourself of the moves.

Most importantly, this book reveals seven key secrets of positive networking. Yes, they must be secrets because most people don't use them.

These secrets are the foundation—the underlying philosophy—of positive networking. Some chapters contain a new secret; others don't. The secrets of positive networking are woven throughout this book; they are the music in the background for the network dance.

LIFE CHANGING

While it may sound like overkill to claim that networking can be life changing, I know from personal experience that it is true. I met Gayle due to her networking (or frog-catching) skills. My life has been greatly enriched by the incredible people I have met and the random and unexpected great experiences that have come my way thanks to the power of networks. Networking is one of the good things you can do in life, so embrace it, enjoy it and give others a chance to meet and know you.

THE FIRST SECRET OF NETWORKING

« You have to kiss a lot of frogs to find a prince. » Positive networking is all about jumping in and getting your feet wet. In the world of frogs, that is a good thing. You have to do a lot of it, and your chances of being a better networker improve the more frogs you meet. You'll happily kiss more frogs and find more princes or princesses.

SUMMARY

frogs, princes & toads

- The seven easy steps to The Network Dance: N.E.T.W.O.R.K. are the skills to be mastered to become a great networker.
- The seven secrets are the conceptual framework and underlying philosophy of positive networking. It's all about attitude.
- We all start out as frogs, but we can move up the frog chain by learning and mastering the network dance and living the secrets.
- Don't rush to categorize contacts by the frog chain. It's for self-assessment. Remember, one person's frog can be another person's prince or princess.
- Kiss more frogs: embrace it, enjoy it, give others a chance to meet and know you.

CHAPTER TWO

networking—the power defined

Too Much Ned

Once upon a time, there was a confident Northern cricket frog named Ned. He thought he was the life of the lily pond. Actually he thought he was a real prince. He would leap from lily pad to lily pad, collecting business cards from everyone and emailing them the very next day.

Ned prided himself on the fact that he could break into any conversation. In his little green brain he was always thinking: "What can you do for me?" Ned got it wrong. He was not a positive networker. Instead, Ned was "alota networker." Alota networker does not a good networker make.

NETWORKING—THE POWER DEFINED

Kissing frogs sounds good in theory, but many of us think of networking as standing around with a glass of wine and a handful of business cards, making small talk with a group of strangers. It is a duty thing, and in the back of your mind, you are thinking:

- Is this the right time to talk about my product?
- When should I hand her my business card?
- These guys look bored talking with me. Maybe I should move on.

What you really want to do is check your watch to see if you can slip away and get back to your real life. Doesn't seem like much fun, does it?

There is a better way. It is found in the secrets of positive networking. And if you don't know what that is, you are about to discover it.

DOING SOMETHING NICE

One night as I was working on this book at home, my nine-year-old daughter Anastasia asked me what I was doing. When I told her, she asked, "What's networking, Dad?"

"It's discovering if you can do something nice for someone else," I replied.

"Oh, that's like paying it forward," she said.

I thought hard about that. Anastasia was right, except that the concept of "paying it forward," taken from the movie of the same name, is about good deeds begetting good deeds. You do something nice for someone and in return ask only that they do something for someone else.

Positive networking embraces this concept and takes it further. Unlike paying it forward, where you do a good deed once and never see the person again, networking is about good things going both ways; it is also about maintaining a connection. It is about the power of networks.

NUGGET

The movie based on the book *Pay it Forward* is about a boy (played by Haley Joel Osment) who decides to make a difference in the world by helping three strangers. All he asks is that those three people each do something nice for three other people. Those nine people must each do something nice for twenty-seven other people and so on. The good deeds continue on, ad infinitum. "Paying it forward" became a world-wide phenomenon.

To better explain what I meant, I said to my daughter, "Remember when Mackenzie was the new girl in school and you went over and talked to her? You knew that she didn't have any friends yet, so you tried to make her feel welcome. Now you've become friends and she is part of your group. You've got more friends, and so does she." It is as simple as that.

When I first tell people that the most powerful secret of positive networking is *discovering what you can do for someone else*, I sometimes get skeptical looks. However, the responses after the idea settles in are quite amazing. An MBA student told me it changed her whole view of networking. "It takes all the pressure off. Now I don't feel I have to go out and sell myself." An accomplished entrepreneur with a well-organized database of twelve thousand contacts, after hearing the secret, called me the very next day and said, "I have always thought of myself as a good networker, but I never looked at it that way. Thank you, what a difference!" Even those who naturally network this way appreciate this philosophy. Many say, "It's the affirmation of what I know to be right."

This secret is what creates and sustains strong personal networks. Welcome to the world of positive networking.

NO HEROICS NEEDED

This doesn't mean you have to become the Mighty Mouse of Networking—"Here I come to save the day!" Simply do some of these things:

- Bring two people together at an event: "Meet Dan. He's a marketing genius; you need to talk with him."

- Rescue a wallflower, or say something sincerely flattering: "I've heard very good things about your company's products."

- Pass on some information or a contact name that would help someone in his endeavors: "I'd like to set up a meeting with a friend of mine who may be able to help you produce your film."

- Tell someone about your product or service if you think it can be of use to him: "Since you do business in Mexico, you might be interested in the online translation services our company offers."

BARRY

One of the best networkers I have met is Barry Appleton. He is one of the leading international trade lawyers in North America with fifty consecutive wins in NAFTA court actions.

Barry is also a member of the World Economic Forum's *Global Leaders for Tomorrow*—a group of up and coming stars under the age of forty. He calls me from his office in Washington, D.C. from time to time to keep in touch. He usually has a fascinating brief on a recent meeting with the President or someone else from inside the Beltway, and he always ends his conversation by saying, "Darcy, now is there anything I can do for you?" And it's not just a platitude. If you ask him for something, he acts on it. Barry is one of the best examples of a person who is always discovering what he can do for someone else.

TOM

Gayle asked Liz Donohue (wife of Tom Donohue, president of the U.S. Chamber of Commerce) what Tom's networking secrets were. Her spontaneous answer was: "He's always trying to help people. If someone needs a job, an introduction, or a doctor for their ailing parents, he'll try and help. That's what he does." Tom is the head of the largest business association in the world and one of the top opinion leaders in America. He uses his vast network of contacts to bring the right people together, from simply introducing an employer to a potential employee to the more complex task of bringing government and business together to change policies.

A PROCESS OF DISCOVERY

Discovering what you can do for someone else is a process of learning about people. It creates natural conversation fire starters and positive energy. Ultimately, you may do nothing more than meet someone and hand out your business card. However, in the back of your mind you should be thinking, "Is there something I might be able to do for this person?"

Don't get me wrong. This discovery process, while altruistic, may mean you sell a product or service through this relationship, but if so, it will come about naturally. It will not be forced. People do business with people they know and trust.

> NUGGET
> The real voyage of discovery consists not of finding new lands, but of seeing the territory with new eyes.
> — Marcel Proust, *Remembrance of Things Past*

Your goal is for people to remember you for all the right reasons. You aren't just making contacts; you are making a real connection and building your reputation.

A DIFFERENT REALITY

In my seminars, I ask, "Who in this audience really enjoys networking?" No more than twenty percent raise their hands. That's it. Eighty percent don't like it. If networking is so wonderful, why this response?

The fact that eighty percent don't like it is shocking. When I delve deeper, I learn that some are uncomfortable doing it, or don't see the value or utility of it. Others just don't believe in it, period. They think networking and networks are just the figment of the imagination of motivational speakers and self-help authors. For them, building networks is more wishful thinking than reality. But revolutionary new research debunks this notion. Networks work.

> NUGGET
> Networking is like broccoli—you may not like broccoli, but deep down you've always known that it was good for you. The same holds true about networking.

THE REVOLUTIONARY SCIENCE OF SMALL WORLDS

In his compelling book, *Nexus: Small Worlds and the Groundbreaking Science of Networks,* Mark Buchanan explores the science of networks and their forms, and chronicles the revolutionary discovery that "the small-worlds idea is one of the newest and most important discoveries in the science."

It all started on a dark and stormy night. Actually, it was a winter's day in the late 1990s when Cornell mathematicians Duncan Watts and Steve Strogatz met to continue Watts's study of small worlds. It's the idea that we are all connected to each other by as few as six handshakes, also known as *six degrees of separation.*

SIX DEGREES OF SEPARATION

The six degrees of separation concept was based on social psychologist Stanley Milgram's well-publicized experiments at Harvard in 1967. His concept was popularized by a movie and play of the same name and the Kevin Bacon Oracle.

We are all familiar with small-world stories—bumping into someone in an airplane who went to the same school as our father, or meeting someone from our hometown in a pub halfway around the world. Unbeknownst to us, Gayle and I lived on the same street, just half a block away from each other, for two years before we were married. These seem like unusual coincidences, but everyone seems to have their own small-world stories. It turns out it is not unusual at all.

NUGGET

Stanley Milgram's small-world research in 1967 showed that social networks were even smaller than imagined. He sent 300 letters to a random selection of people in Nebraska and Kansas. Their task: to get the letter to a stockbroker in Boston using only personal contacts. Milgram found it took an average of only six contacts to get this letter to the stockbroker—hence the saying, "six degrees of separation."

NUGGET

Type the name of any actor into the Kevin Bacon Oracle website, *www.cs.virginia.edu/oracle/* and try to connect him to Kevin Bacon—either through the movies the two of them have been in together (a Kevin Bacon number of one) or through a movie he has been in with someone else who has been in a movie with Kevin. Confused? Here's an example. Brendan Fraser was in *Twenty Bucks* with Elisabeth Shue who was in *Hollow Man* with Kevin Bacon. Brendan is connected to Kevin by two degrees of separation. On average, there are only three degrees of separation (not even six) between any actor and Kevin Bacon.

CONNECT THE DOTS

Using mathematical graph theory, Watts and Strogatz began connecting dots on paper, searching for an answer to the small-worlds phenomenon. A few months later, Buchanan reports they "connected their dots in a peculiar way that no mathematician had ever envisioned, and in so doing stumbled over a graph of an unprecedented and fascinating kind." Their findings stunned the research community, and they were inundated with queries from scientists around the world. It was revolutionary stuff.

SIXTY MILLION HANDSHAKES

Watts and Strogatz found that a somewhat orderly pattern of linkages between dots, with just a dash of random connections, made for a very powerful network. It was these random connections that caused the path from one point to another to shrink amazingly.

If you look at social networks, for example, it is safe to assume that everyone has a network of contacts. For simplicity, assume that everyone has a network of fifty contacts—friends, colleagues, acquaintances. Assume that each of these contacts has their own network of fifty people, and so on. Now imagine that all of these people are connected to each other, like a huge fishnet cast around the world, until all six billion people are connected. It would take *sixty million* connections or handshakes to make contact with someone halfway around the world.

Now, for every ten thousand people in that six billion, introduce just two additional random connections—or shortcuts—between any two people. Here is where the power of a small world gets spooky and the magic begins. With this addition of only two random shortcuts per ten thousand people, it now takes only *eight handshakes* to meet someone halfway around the world. Not eight *million*—*eight*, period.

Add a third random shortcut, and the handshakes drop to five. Watts and Strogatz proved this startling fact mathematically, and in doing so discovered the answer to the small-worlds phenomenon that had eluded scientists for three hundred years. Milgram's six degrees of separation was thus proven to be true: Fewer than six handshakes could connect all the six billion people on the planet. Walt Disney was right: It's a small world after all. Welcome to the magic kingdom.

NUGGET

Duncan Watts, in his book, *Small Worlds, The Dynamics of Networks between Order and Randomness*, reports, "Since the first published version of this work appeared in the journal *Nature* (1998), Steve Strogatz and I have been contacted by dozens of researchers from virtually every discipline (yes, including English literature), who have all been struck by the relevance of small-world networks to something in their field of expertise."

WHAT THIS MEANS TO US

What does all this mean to us, in a practical sense? It means that if we want to participate in the power of networks, we have to go out and connect the dots for ourselves. We have to meet real people. In Malcolm Gladwell's bestseller, *The Tipping Point: How Little Things Can Make a Big Difference*, he states, "Six degrees of separation doesn't mean that everyone is linked to everyone else in just six steps. It means that a very small number of people are linked to everyone else in a few steps and the rest of us are linked to the world through those special few." Our goal is to become one of those special few, the great networkers.

That said, there is more to come. The science behind networks gets better—for you, the networker.

THE STRENGTH OF WEAK TIES

It turns out that our weak contacts, even distant acquaintances, are often more powerful forces in our network than close friends. Even before Watts and Strogatz pieced together their mathematical proof of the power of small worlds, Mark Granovetter of Johns Hopkins University researched the "strength of weak ties" in social networks. He discovered that more than eighty percent of the time, people who find jobs through networking find them through weak connections—acquaintances rather than close friends. This was a startling revelation.

This means all our contacts are important. Why? Because our personal network is connected to myriad networks through contacts near and far, strong and weak. Because of the brilliant randomness of it all—because networks operate somewhere in the ether between order and chaos—we never really know when a given contact will be important. All the more reason to stay plugged in, to engage in the network dance and treat all contacts like gold.

NUGGET

In 1973, Mark Granovetter published a classic paper on "The strength of weak ties." In his study, he interviewed individuals who had been able to get a new job as a result of a connection through a friend or acquaintance. He learned that 84% of these people found their jobs through the weak link connections, people they saw only once in a blue moon. Ongoing research has supported this concept. Those weak links—acquaintances—may be the most powerful connections in your network.

THE SCIENCE AND THE ART

While networking is an art, it's impossible to overlook the groundbreaking science that proves the power of networks and the small worlds they create. What can you do with the knowledge that you are only six handshakes away from anyone in the world? Start by recognizing the following:

- Good things happen to good networkers—accept it.
- The small-worlds phenomenon happens all the time—expect it.
- Your network is always on—tap into it.

RICK

Good things happen to good networkers—accept it. At forty-one, Rick Turner was the youngest chairman in the history of The Board of Trade. He thinks he's just a frog—but in reality, he's way up the frog chain. At a conference we attended together, he told Gayle and me about some of the amazing things that had come his way lately, seemingly out of the blue. He had been invited to sit on some prominent boards, participate in a series of high-level international gatherings and tour the U.S. Space Command under Cheyenne Mountain in Colorado Springs. And, he had just been appointed chairman of a billion-dollar public corporation. In his modest and self-deprecating way, he said, "Darcy, I don't really know how this all happened."

My reply was easy. "I do. It's the strange and random good things that come to those who are contributors. It's what happens when you participate in your community and volunteer your time and energy. You have built an incredible network, and it works."

Like most Board of Trade chairs, Rick has been active for a number of years, both within his industry and as a volunteer in the community. He has served on hospital and police foundation boards, he attends a dozen charity events a year as a matter of routine and he has been the volunteer chair of two major business associations. Rick has unwittingly plugged himself into an amazing network. He's not just a *participant*; he's a *contributor*. In positive networks, the current goes both ways.

MAUREEN

Small-worlds phenomena occur all the time—expect it. During a break at a three-day conference in Mexico, I began a conversation with a gentleman from Korea seated behind me. Minutes later, I spoke to the woman in the seat in front of me. When I asked her for a card, she told me she had brought only three. Maureen was an economist from Washington, D.C. and well established in her career, so perhaps she didn't think she needed to carry cards? I introduced Maureen to my new Korean acquaintance, whereupon she learned that he knew her husband very well.

Later, Maureen said to me, "Wasn't that amazing?" My response: "That is exactly what I would expect."

Although thousands of miles separated Maureen from the Korean gentleman, I looked at it another way—only two handshakes separated them. I suspect Maureen carries more cards these days. She seemed excited by the magic of small worlds. If we know we are only six handshakes away from anyone on the globe, a world of possibilities lies before us.

SOMETIMES IT GETS SPOOKY

What we learn is that small-world connections are not so unique after all. But sometimes it can get downright spooky.

While a sophomore at McGill, I traveled to the West Coast one summer to complete officer training as an army engineer. Westbound, my aircraft got laid up in Winnipeg, the Prairie city where I was born and lived until the age of two. I hadn't been back since. I needed a place to stay for the night, so I phoned a classmate and close friend, David Farmer. "Come on over," David responded. "I'm sure my landlady won't mind. Tell the cab driver the address is 944 Somerville Avenue."

David's landlady, Dr. Borthwick-Leslie, turned out to be a welcoming and fascinating person—the first woman graduate of the faculty of medicine in Winnipeg.

After half an hour of chatting over a cup of tea, she asked, "Was your father invalided in the army and sent back to Winnipeg from England at the end of the Second World War?"

"Yes," I replied.

"Come with me," she said, escorting me to the back porch. "Do you see that small handle at the bottom of the screen door? Your father put that on so that you and your two brothers could open it. You lived in this house until you were two years old. I bought this house from your father when your family moved to Montreal."

The good doctor made me feel right "at home" that night.

YVES

Networks are always on; they're humming in the background. Sometimes we forget this and go it alone, struggling to make contacts and connections when all we need to do is tap into our network.

When Yves Potvin, the founder of Yves Veggie Cuisine, organized a year-long education program for the Young Presidents' Organization (YPO), his mission was to come up with a spectacular program of speakers and events that would benefit all members. So he sent out a personal letter to YPO members telling them what he wanted to achieve and asking for their thoughts.

He was flooded with a remarkable list of speakers from every walk of life, who were now just a phone call away. Yves discovered he had tapped into a group already wired into many networks. He flipped the switch and experienced a power surge.

NETWORK SHEPA

Networking requires an ethos of awareness. Tibetans call consciousness, or awareness, *shepa.* Positive networkers have a highly developed sense of *network shepa.* They are aware of the value of building and maintaining social networks, both collectively and individually. Not only are they conscious of positive networking; they facilitate it by initiating a conversation, by graciously bringing others into a group and by listening and following up. They champion networking.

THE SECOND SECRET OF NETWORKING

The second secret of positive networking, « **discovering what you can do for someone else,** » is the cornerstone philosophy of positive networking. Science has shown us that networks happen whether we like it or not, and it's up to us to decide how powerful and positive ours will be.

And it all starts so simply—by introducing ourselves and exchanging business cards. Let the networking begin!

SUMMARY

networking—the power defined

- Discovering what you can do for someone else is the most fundamental principle of positive networking. Thinking this way takes all the pressure off.
- Good things happen to good networkers and those they touch—because of what they put into their relationships.
- The small-worlds phenomenon is real. An opportunity to reach someone half way around the world is less than six handshakes from you. This opens up a world of possibilities.
- Do not underestimate the value of weak connections, which can be even more powerful than strong ones.
- Your network is always on; keep it charged. Meeting a contact can light up a whole substation of contacts or you can experience a power surge when powerful networks connect.
- The best way to keep your network charged is to have high *network shepa*—an awareness of the value of building and maintaining social networks.

N

CHAPTER THREE

never leave home without them

Jeremiah Was a Networking Bullfrog

Once upon a time, Jeremiah, a middle-management bullfrog, received an email from his boss, Freddie Flycatcher, requesting that he come along to a business reception at the Insect Inn. Jeremiah was thrilled. This was his chance to really impress his boss with his networking skills.

At the event, Jeremiah steered clear of the swamp water and fly canapés and spent his time meeting as many other frogs as he could. He was doing great. Jeremiah's boss spotted him and brought him over to meet a very important contact.

"Marsha, I'd like you to meet Jeremiah, he's our top webware salesman. Jeremiah, give Marsha your card."

Jeremiah reached into his pocket, and came up empty.

NEVER LEAVE HOME WITHOUT THEM

The American Express commercial says it all. Never leave home without your cards—your business cards, that is. Everyone knows that they need business cards and should give them out. Too obvious, you say? Half the people I meet in North America don't have business cards on them.

"I forgot to bring cards."

"I could kick myself; I left them in my desk."

"Gee, I thought I brought some; they must be in here somewhere."

It gets even more amazing. When they do have cards on them, half the time they don't give them out. How do I know this? After I give out my card, about half the people I meet return the favor only after I ask. And, they seem relieved that I've asked. While there are exceptions, it seems in this hemisphere, the exchange of business cards is a hit and miss affair.

> **NUGGET**
> If you leave home without your business cards—go back and get them. Yes, they are that important.

CARD-FREE ZONE

An invitation Gayle and I received for an international business reception and dinner in Washington State made it clear that people were supposed to network. People from various economic regions of the continent had been invited with the express purpose of doing business with each other. What happened? More than half the people we met didn't have business cards. Their excuses ranged from "I gave my last card to your wife," to "Let me see; I may have a card in my wallet. Hope you don't mind if it's a bit dog-eared."

It went from bad to worse. Before we sat down to

NUGGET

Place cards should have names printed on both sides and be large enough to read across the table. Turn your place card around if it is printed on only one side. You know your own name, so give others at the table some help.

dinner at our table of eight, Gayle and I walked around the table, introduced ourselves and gave out our business cards. I received cards from a couple of people; the rest just mumbled their names. I couldn't confirm their names by looking at a nametag—they didn't have one. I glanced at the place cards on the table, but the handwriting was so small it was no help.

I felt forced to fish this information out of my tablemates, and hoped that I didn't stick my foot in my mouth during the process.

MENTAL BLOCK

What mental block keeps people from bringing and handing out business cards? When I ask my seminar participants this question, I get some quick retorts:

- "I don't know why, I just don't think about bringing them."
- "It feels pushy, like a sell job."
- "It's kind of tacky."

The negative comments about "sell jobs" and "too pushy" come from bad experiences. Most of us have been handed a business card and subjected to the big sell job—the fax blasts and emails can't be far behind. While memorable—for all the wrong reasons—this misuse of the business card is thankfully rare. This is *not* what positive networking is about.

The more common reason that people don't bring and give out business cards is low *network shepa.* The use of business cards is simply not on their radar screen. They leave home or the office without them, and when they get to the event they leave them in their pockets even as they are making their introductions.

There could be another reason that people don't hand out their business cards—because they have been advised not to in networking books and pamphlets. I must respectfully disagree. Giving out your business card serves one purpose—letting people know who you are. It's that simple. Being aware of this, you'll be more inclined to hand out your card.

MAKE IT A HABIT

In many cultures, particularly Asia, handing out your card is a natural part of the introduction process. There's none of the anxiety of wondering *if* you should hand your card to a person or *when* you should do it. My theory is why not give out your card to someone you don't know when you first meet them? Of course, there may be exceptions when discretion suggests waiting until a bit later in the conversation, but the general rule is, do it right away. There's no better time. You'll be surprised how handing out your card prompts others to do the same.

If handing out your card seems like a logical thing to do, introducing yourself by name would seem like a no-brainer, but many people don't tell you their name. You introduce yourself to someone: "Hello, I'm Darcy Rezac." The person shakes your hand, smiles and replies: "Hi, nice to meet you." (Last time I checked, "Nicetomeetyou" wasn't a name.)

Introducing yourself by your first and last name is part of the mannerly ritual of introductions. It's also the first step in personal branding.

IT'S YOUR BRAND

Business cards are part of your personal and corporate branding, so card appearance is important. After nearly two decades I have seen every kind imaginable: cards with printing so small you can't read them without a magnifying glass, fold-over cards with tear-off coupons, oversized cards, undersized cards, wooden cards, business-card CD-ROM disks, cards with photos and cards that dispense dental floss.

I carried aluminum business cards when I worked for Alcan, a multinational aluminum company. People still talk about this memorable card.

I've been handed cards that run the gamut from gold embossed with the title "Ambassador Extraordinaire and Plenipotentiary" (which is not a joke) to flimsy black and white insta-print (the latter from the mayor of a world-class city).

My favorite card was Mary Robinson's—a card that simply stated, "Mary Robinson, President of Ireland." Now that's a "don't call me, I'll call you" card.

KEEP IT SIMPLE

There are all kinds of innovative card ideas, and the do's and don'ts of business-card design can be overwhelming. These three simple tests will serve you well:

- Business Card Eye Test: Are people able to read the information on your card in low light?
- Field of Nowhere Test: Is the information on your card captured correctly—without corrections—in a card scanner?
- When in Rome Test: Do your cards work in other cultures?

BUSINESS CARD EYE TEST

After having given out more than 30,000 business cards in my career (and receiving back about 20,000), I have seen what most cards have in common: the typeface is too small. In many cases the information on the card is unreadable, especially in the low light of receptions or dinners.

Frog Hollow
Hotels and Resorts
FH

MICHAEL P. BULLRUSH
Senior Vice President / General Manager

300-888 Wet Place, Pondville, WA USA
DID 425-888-2869, Tel 425-665-9588, Fax 425-665-9599, Cell 425-825-9363
E-mail mbullrush@froghollow.com

This is a very typical card, but I've frequently seen the person's name in even smaller type. If you can read this actual size card in low light, congratulations; you are probably under forty years old. Otherwise, you most likely have presbyopia: "short arm" syndrome. Your arms just aren't long enough to hold that card far enough out to read it. "Short arm" syndrome affects a large portion of the population. You want these people to be able to read your card, no matter what your twenty-something graphic designer tells you.

» Business Card Eye Test

Ask seven friends to rate your card, including some over forty, and do it in low light. As though they are meeting you for the first time, ask them:

- Can you read my name?
- Can you read my title?
- Can you read my company name?
- Can you read my contact information?

NUGGET

Presbyopia is not a disease. It is a slow, natural part of the aging process, though it seems to happen overnight when you hit your mid-forties. Early warning signs include blurred vision when you are trying to read small print. You start holding menus, phone books and medicine bottles way, way out to get them into focus. Eventually, your arm isn't long enough. Sorry, but it is now time for reading glasses or bifocals (an invention of Benjamin Franklin).

THE FIELD OF NOWHERE TEST

Card scanners are handy little devices that capture the information contained on business cards and organize it into the correct fields in an address database—with no typing. More and more people are using card scanners to organize their business cards in their email computer databases.

» Field of Nowhere Test

Put your card through a card scanner.

- Do both your name and email address go into the correct fields?
- Better yet, does all your information flow into the proper fields?

If it doesn't, you may end up being a glitch in someone's database. You won't get on their Christmas card list, or any other list for that matter. I don't bother to correct a scanning error unless it is a contact with whom I have already bonded. All my cards go through my *CardScan.* If my card scanner likes them, so do I.

FITTING INTO THE PACK

Cards that may work well in North America as "creative" designs may not work in other cultures. My advice is to fit into the pack. For example, in France, a clever card won't be taken seriously. Some Asian countries use larger cards, and others use cards that are so lightweight that North Americans would consider them flimsy.

» When in Rome Test

If you are doing business in another country, ask someone with experience in that culture to critique your card. Ask them:

- Does my card pass the cross-cultural test?

Do your homework and be culturally aware; it's part of your *network shepa.*

PERSONAL BRANDING

You've got a card that has passed the readability test, the card scan test and the culture test; what else is of utmost importance when it comes to card design?

Not only is your name part of your personal branding, so is your title. Make sure you put it on your card and in a large enough point size.

Your professional designation is part of your personal

branding. Company policy may dictate whether it appears on your card or not. Established and well-known individuals may choose not to show their designation or university credentials. My advice is not to hide your light under a bushel. Here are some simple rules to follow about your designation:

- If it helps others understand what you do and provides an additional level of confidence in your ability, use it.
- If you are just starting out in business, use it.
- If you can't decide if you should use it, err on the side of using it. Don't be shy.

Put the name you want to be called on your business card. If you don't expect to be addressed as P.T., then don't list initials only on your card. (If you are P.T. Barnum, then by all means, do.)

If your company requires you to put your initials on your card, add to them the name you want to be called. Example: P.T. (Peter) Reed. The same is true if your name is Daniel, but everyone calls you Dan. Put Daniel (Dan) on your card. Make it easy for people to call you by your name.

PhD (FAILED)

One of the most unusual designations I ever saw was on the business card of a fellow from India. After his name were the words, "Ph.D. (failed)." Intrigued, I asked him what that meant. He said he wanted people to know that he had been smart enough to get accepted into a difficult Ph.D. program, even though he had not obtained the degree. Interesting concept, but I don't think it would fly in North America.

CORPORATE BRANDING

Just as important as personal branding is reinforcing your corporate branding. We've already established that point size on business cards needs to be bigger, and there's more information on cards with web sites and other contact information for mobile devices.

Use all the real estate available. The flip side of your card is a great place to brand your company. Repeat your company logo or display your company web site, slogan or business description. People often use more color on this side of their card for greater impact.

NUGGET

Light color type is very popular but it can make reading your card even more difficult.

CARD OF MANY USES

Two-sided cards are also useful if you have a volunteer position, such as a member on the board of the local children's hospital or United Way. I am an honorary naval captain, and I have that information printed on the other side of a special version of my business card. If you are doing business in a country with a foreign language, a two-sided card is a good idea. In Asia, this is a necessity.

NUGGET

In Asia when you have your cards prepared, have someone who knows you personally check that the nuances of your name are translated correctly. They may give you a name that fits your personality, or make your name work phonetically.

A CARD IN THE HAND

People often say, "I haven't got my card yet, I'm still working on my logo" or "I haven't gotten around to printing cards." My advice: Any card is better than no card. Use a graphic designer, by all means, but stick to your guns about

POP QUIZ

When was the last time you redid your business cards?

point size. Another good solution is to go to a printing house that specializes in business card printing. They have people on staff to design your card quickly. Just remember to do the three tests before you print your cards.

Want to print your own card from your computer? It's easy to create a good-looking card ready for immediate use; just make sure it doesn't look amateurish. Follow our guidelines in the appendix.

HOW MANY CARDS TO CARRY?

Now that you've got a card that people can read, and that you are proud to hand out, how many of these fine looking cards should you carry? I use the rule of sevens. Carry an "emergency" minimum of seven cards at all times. At business luncheons or breakfasts, most tables seat eight, so you need a minimum of seven cards.

However, more cards are required to work the "pond" before and after the event. Take a minimum of twenty-eight, in keeping with multiples of seven. If this seven stuff doesn't work for you, just take a big bundle.

KEEP A STASH

Be like a squirrel—stash cards everywhere—at your home and office, in your briefcase, car, tracksuit and workout bag. That way you'll take them everywhere.

Keep a well-stocked supply of cards on hand. Order at least two boxes at a time. Turn the cards around three quarters of the way through each box as a reminder to re-order. Turning one card won't do it, because you usually grab a bundle.

If you are going to a conference, take two boxes of cards and pack them separately. Your luggage may be lost or delayed, and there you'll be, up a creek without a card. Not every town has a 24-hour Kinko's to churn out temporary cards.

NUGGET

Keep a copy of the digital file for your business cards on your computer. That way, when you need new cards you have the artwork readily available.

WHO GETS A BUSINESS CARD?

For most organizations, everyone should have business cards. It's "so last millennium" to provide business cards only for selected employees. Give everyone in your organization a business card, then train them how to use them effectively.

When I asked Danny Sitnam, president of Helijet International Inc. (the largest scheduled helicopter carrier in North America), who in his organization got business cards, he said, "Everybody—I want everyone to network." Danny gets it; he has high *network shepa.*

EMPLOYMENT WANTED

People who need business cards the most are the job seekers. Frequently they come to see if I can connect them with someone, yet they come without business cards. Are they hesitant to prepare a card because they are unsure of what to put as their "title?"

Why not establish credentials based on prior work experience? "Consultant" is a catch-all, but some people find it too generic. Someone employed as a human relations manager can use Human Relations Advisor. An information technology worker can state their area of expertise such as Database Management Specialist. A professional designation can be helpful.

Remember "the strength of weak ties" when looking for a job. Use all your contacts, even acquaintances. Make it easy for people to get in touch with you, preferably on a line your kids won't answer. A cellular phone number and an email address can put you in circulation. If you do not give people an easy way to get in touch with you, how can they help you?

CALLING CARDS FOR THE 21ST CENTURY

Too often, people who aren't in the everyday work world think they shouldn't have a card. Who made up that rule? In Victorian times, men and women carried calling cards with their name and address.

From the collection of R. Vreeken.

Calling cards are still a good idea. Networking is about meeting new people and developing new relationships, so why not create a card to improve the process? Just make sure you use the same design rules as for business cards. Besides, personal cards are just useful. Pulling out a personal card is certainly easier than spelling out all the information to someone filling out a form. "It's Thomson, without a 'p.'"

If it's easier for you to give out a personal card in a social setting than a business card, do that. The point is, don't be afraid to give out a card.

RETIRED?

When people retire today, many continue in business pursuits. A retired friend, who sits as a director on many boards and is well known in the community, has a very simple card with his name and contact information. This is an "emeritus" card: a professionally printed, black and white card with elegant raised letters that subtly indicates its owner is not in the rat race anymore, but still a player.

Retired folks, who don't have or need emeritus status, sometimes print up cards with humor. Gayle met this fine gentleman over coffee in the breakfast room at the Howard Johnson in Helena, Montana. His card read: "Somewhat Retired Livestock Buyer."

Phone 357 - 3600
Area Code 406

RUSSELL L. BENSON
Somewhat Retired Livestock Buyer

CHINOOK, MONTANA 59523

P.O. Box 1299 515 Missouri

YOU ARE NEVER TOO OLD

Even Judy's eighty-something mother has business cards. Judy made them for her when she was moving from her family home to a new apartment. Her mom is a bit of a tea granny, so Judy downloaded clipart of a little teapot and cups for the card. Mrs. Thomson proudly pulled her cards out of her wallet to let friends know she had moved and they would be coming to a new address for tea and card games. This is a woman who worked most of her life but never had business cards. You are never too old to get business cards and use them.

CEDRIC

Who gives out a business card and gets a medal for it? Actually, it was two medals and it was my great friend Cedric Steele, community leader and networking prince. A few years ago, he hosted a dinner for senior American naval officers at the famous Empress Hotel in his hometown of Victoria, Canada. Cedric handed his business card to his guest, four-star Admiral Archie Clemins, commander in chief of the U.S. Pacific Fleet, and the Admiral reciprocated. During the course of the evening, the Admiral thanked Cedric for his hospitality and then asked, "Cedric, is there anything I can do for you?"

"There is, Admiral," Cedric responded. "The people of Victoria have never had the honor of hosting one of your aircraft carriers for a port visit."

An aircraft carrier visit is a huge request at the best of times, but given Victoria's shallow harbor, this was a particularly ambitious request. A flurry of emails and phone calls ensued, finally reaching the desk of the U.S. Chief of Naval Operations. A week later, Cedric received an email from Pearl Harbor. It simply said, "Cedric, the *Abe* is coming in February—Archie."

The visit of the U.S.S. *Abraham Lincoln* was both a huge success and the start of an annual aircraft carrier port call to Victoria. That simple business card exchange brought millions of much-needed dollars to Victoria during its low season, and the city became a favorite port of call with U.S. sailors. The United States Navy awarded Cedric two medals for making it all happen.

Sometimes you just have to hand out your business card and ask for the impossible.

THE THIRD SECRET OF NETWORKING

The third secret of positive networking is a practical one. And it must be a secret, because so few people do it. « **Introduce yourself by name, always carry business cards and give them out. Make it a habit.** » You'll find it's a worthwhile habit.

SUMMARY

never leave home without them

- Have a minimum of seven cards with you at all times and **we really mean at ALL times**. You can never carry too many cards, only too few.
- Introduce yourself by name when you meet people and give them your card.
- If necessary, have both business and personal cards.
- If you don't have a job, you really need a business card.
- If you are retired or "stay at home," have a personal card.
- Make your cards memorable but easy to read. We're all getting older. Do the Business Card Eye Test.
- Put your card through a card scanner and do the Field of Nowhere Test.
- If you are doing business in another country, do the When in Rome Test to make sure your card is culturally acceptable.

E

CHAPTER FOUR

the four E's—establish, extend, exchange, engage

Leap Frog

Once upon a time, Emeril and Olive Hopper were invited to an important business dinner. Olive was top frog—CEO—of one of the leading environmental engineering companies in the Western Wetlands. Emeril, an affable pobblebonk frog, was her husband. He knew the host, Mr. Newt, was having some serious "green" issues with his drilling company. Emeril thought a new safety product, developed by Olive's company, would end the Greenpeace boycott of Mr. Newt's company.

Emeril took Olive over to greet Mr. Newt and before Emeril could introduce Olive properly, Mr. Newt absentmindedly shook her hand, while beginning to speak to the person beside her. Olive knew exactly where Mr. Newt fit in the frog chain, and it wasn't "prince." Although it may have been a coincidence, Olive entered into an exclusive licensing agreement with Mr. Newt's competition.

THE FOUR E'S—ESTABLISH, EXTEND, EXCHANGE, ENGAGE

The Four E's—*establish* eye contact, *extend* your hand, *exchange* business cards and then *engage* in conversation—are the first steps in making a good impression. Yet we see people getting tripped up by simple things time and time again. Sometimes it's just one small thing, such as not making eye contact. That's easy to fix. Other times it is much more jarring.

There are "close encounters with toads." That's when you're introduced to someone, and as he or she is shaking your hand, they look right past you to find a "more important" person. Or there's the "what am I, chopped liver?" experience. That's when someone leans across the table and gives his card to the husband, but not the wife.

JUDGING A BOOK BY ITS COVER

Good networkers don't assume anything; they never judge a book by its cover. When people put a label on someone, they close doors to possibilities.

At a European conference with some of the world's most high-powered "suits," I glimpsed a funky-looking guy with dreadlocks and sandals standing in the middle of the crowd. As it turned out, he was Jaron Lanier, the brilliant father of "virtual reality." He is not only a computer scientist, but a composer, visual artist and author. Meeting this interesting guy was one of the highlights of the conference.

JACKIE O

Some people have natural social graces. When Jackie

Kennedy greeted people, she had the ability to make them feel they were the most important person in the world. It was how she spoke directly to you, her eye contact, her total concentration on the gems of wisdom spewing forth from your mouth, and her intimate, whisper-like way of responding to what you said.

EYE CONTACT COUNTS

Making and keeping eye contact is the first step to establishing a strong connection with another person. In Western cultures, a person who doesn't look you straight in the eye makes a poor impression, and sometimes it's considered downright rude. If you look people in the eye in a friendly manner, it shows you are interested in them. You get their attention. That's important to establishing a foothold for an ongoing conversation.

SPACE FILLER SYNDROME

Has the "space filler syndrome" ever happened to you? While talking with someone, you get the sense your conversation mate is not giving you his full attention. It's a classic bad-networking technique, the way he nods and looks like he is listening to you, while scanning the room for someone more important, hoping you won't notice. Wrong. People notice. Always give one hundred percent of your attention—just like Jackie O.

WHY AM I SMILING?

Positive networking starts with a smile, a universal communication signal. You smile at someone; they smile back. It's automatic. The brain is hard-wired to function this way. You can't help yourself; it goes back to caveman days, when it was a mechanism for survival. A smile opens the door to friendly communication.

Early one Saturday morning, Judy and her friend Carol, who was visiting from Australia, were walking along the seawall in Vancouver's Stanley Park. Most people they passed were lost in their own thoughts, brows furrowed, eyes staring blankly into the space in front of them.

"Gee, people aren't very friendly here," said Carol. "Let's try something and see what happens." In her perky Aussie accent, Carol began to belt out a "Good morning!" and smile at everyone they passed. Pretty soon, Judy and Carol were inundated with startled smiles and belated, cheerful "Good mornings." Try it sometime. It will become infectious.

HANDSHAKE CHALLENGE

When someone smiles, makes eye contact with you and extends his hand, it's nice to get a firm, dry handshake in return. In Western cultures, any other kind of handshake can pigeonhole a person in a negative way. There's the classic limp-fish handshake—cold, lifeless and weak. A variation is the clutch, when you get just the person's fingertips. What? They are afraid of palm-on-palm contact?

Network shepa means being conscious of your handshake; make it a good one. Give your kids a hand up with this special skill. From an early age, teach them to shake hands when they meet people. It will become second nature to them.

NUGGET

Different countries have different styles of handshakes. Some Asians have a very gentle handshake. People from other countries shake hands vigorously, often several times, while still others indulge in only one up and down motion.

PRACTICE MAKES PERFECT

For most people a sweaty handshake can be cured. It's usually just nervousness. The solution: The more networking you do, the more comfortable you become, the drier your palms. If you have sweaty palms, carry a hanky and wipe your hands frequently.

THE GERM NETWORK

Since handshaking is such a big part of networking, I tell people in my networking courses to keep a wet wipe package in their pocket. This is particularly important for networkers eating finger foods or sitting down to dinner right after a reception. It's not that I have a Howard Hughes cleanliness phobia, but shaking hands spreads germs. For events that I host, I have the hotel or restaurant provide warm towels to the head table guests after a heavy round of handshaking.

NUGGET

A medical condition affecting one percent of the population, called *hyperhydrosis*, is caused by hyperactive sympathetic nervous activity in the sweat glands of the hands. There is surgical treatment for the condition. It proves there are cases where practice doesn't make perfect.

TO KISS OR NOT TO KISS

To kiss or not to kiss can be a dilemma when close friends meet in a business situation. Do I kiss them or shake their hand? If you would normally hug or kiss in a personal situation, then hug or kiss them. Avoid big bear hugs and kisses on the lips.

The other popular form of "face time" is the cheek-to-cheek kiss, but it's a tricky one. A person leans over and gives you a stylish air kiss. Once that happens, you are committed.

You do the left, right...but wait, they are back on the left. Is this ever going to end? Relax, that's the European style. Most North Americans do their own version of this: left cheek, then right cheek. When in doubt, just follow the other person's lead.

POP QUIZ

Don't know what kind of handshake you have? Test yourself. Shake hands with people you know and have them rate you.

WHEN IN ROME

The concept of personal space differs around the world. In some countries, people stand very close to each other when they are introduced (close enough to feel each other's breath). Even if you find it uncomfortable, you should not move away from the person, as this could be insulting.

When you are networking in a cross-cultural environment, arm yourself with as much information as you can, and ensure it's up to date. *The CultureGram*™ series and web sites such as *executiveplanet.com* and *learnaboutcultures.com* are easy ways to get up to speed on cultural and business etiquette. Equally important is to tap into your network of people on the ground in a specific country.

EXCHANGING CARDS

The four E's are a lesson in serious multi-tasking. As you are making eye contact, extend your hand, reach into your pocket, give out a business card and introduce yourself by name. Not much could go wrong with that, right? Wrong. People haphazardly hand you a card as if it was a stick of chewing gum, or after receiving your card, they stuff it in their pocket without a glance.

While this is typically unintentional, it's impolite.

Acknowledge any business card you receive—look at it, read it, make a comment based on it. In some cultures, business card exchanges are regarded as a high art. In all cultures, it's a very important activity.

YOUR BEST CARD CASE

Business card cases are great to keep your cards clean, but when you get to a networking event, you want your cards to be easily accessible. Fishing a card out of a cardholder takes too long. That's why the best card-carrying case is your left jacket pocket and your best dispenser is your left hand. Women may not always wear a jacket, but before they enter the room, they can put a stack of cards in their left hand and use it as a card dispenser.

NUGGET

Make sure the card you hand out is yours. Use one pocket for collecting cards, and the other pocket for your supply of cards.

QUICK DRAW MCGRAW?

I have always prided myself on having cards in an easily accessible pocket for a quick draw. Men are fortunate to have a small card pocket on the left-hand lower inside of their jacket. That's the pocket I used until a fateful event.

I was in Japan, meeting with a group of high-level government officials. We all bowed to one another while my sidekick, Wilf Wakely, filmed this momentous occasion for posterity. I reached into my lower inside card pocket and with substantial flair pulled out a stack of cards that went flying around the room.

My performance was even more embarrassing because proffering a business card in Japan carries heavy protocol, second only to the ancient tea ceremony. Few people on earth value networking more than the Japanese. Here is a little primer on the art of networking, Japanese style, from my colleague, Wilf.

NETWORKING IN JAPAN—VERY HIGH *SHEPA*

"Business progress in Japan, like anywhere else, is about getting to know new people. For the Japanese, getting to know new people is trickier, given that it's a vertically oriented society. In Japan, waltzing into someone's office and saying, 'Hi, wanna do business?' is not a route to success. Either someone you know knows someone who will introduce you, or you have to find another way.

The Japanese have a very high level of networking awareness. They hold specific networking events in September and January, typically hosted by the local chamber of commerce or a trade association. These involve a cast of hundreds, a few speeches, then—*wham*—it's time to meet folks.

The most essential tool in this process is the business card, or *meishi.* The *meishi* identifies the bearer's company and position. Without these two essentials, it is almost impossible to speak to someone, lest one risk committing an irredeemable faux pas. In ancient times, all of this would have been immediately apparent from the dress (armour), company (retainers with very big swords) and circumstances (you are in *his* castle). In modern times, where everyone wears the same suit, the *meishi* has become indispensable.

Guidebooks about Japan jam the shelves of the book shops at most leading hotels in Tokyo, right beside the toothpaste, razors and dental floss. Many of the guidebook writers, wanting to leave nothing to doubt, have adopted a scientific approach to the fine art of proffering business cards—something like,

> **NUGGET**
> In Asia it is rude to write on someone's business card in that person's presence.

'Receive the *meishi* with a hand on each side while bending forward from the waist approximately forty degrees; carefully examine the card before placing it in your *meishi* folder. Reaching into your pile and again, with both hands, offer your own to your opposite party, making sure that you proffer the card right side up so the receiver can read it.' Try that with a plate of sushi and a tiny cup of hot *sake* in your hands.

Here is what I think—and I have gone through this hundreds of times. Don't get hung up on the science of passing out *meishi*. Remember only this: The other guy's *meishi* represents him and his company. Don't snatch it out of his hand and drop it in your side pocket. Look at it; say something admiring—be nice. When you hand your own out, remember that it too represents your company and how you fit in it. Don't spray them about the room, as my friend, Darcy, has been known to do. You are not feeding geese."

WHEN AND WHERE

At organized business or networking events, hand out your card immediately. The rules aren't so cut and dried when it comes to social events, such as parties and family functions. But all functions and encounters are network-building opportunities, and all contacts can be important. Try and find an appropriate opportunity to exchange cards, and the sooner the better. Yes, people network at weddings, barbeques and in the movie line-up. Remember John Hunter?

The trick is to remember to bring cards. You can't give them out if you don't have them.

A GENTLE NUDGE

Sometimes attendees of events need to be nudged to exchange cards. When I first joined my organization, I noticed that people sitting at tables would introduce themselves only to the people on either side of them, and sometimes they would give out their card, sometimes not. These days, I ensure that at all our events, the master of ceremonies tells the audience, "We have a tradition at The Board of Trade of exchanging business cards." The emcee asks everyone to take out their business cards and introduce themselves to everyone at their table. Then things start happening. A real buzz fills the room. In fact, it gets so loud that we make sure the business card exchange happens just before the meal is served, or it is difficult to secure the crowd's attention again. People with low *network shepa* may need a gentle nudge to give out their cards.

NAME CALLING

Engaging anyone in conversation involves asking questions, being interested and staying focused. You need a good introduction and conversational firestarters, and sometimes you have to bring out the heavy equipment—icebreakers.

Start with the easiest and most charming technique—call people by their names. Why? It helps you remember the person's name and it helps others around you remember the person's name. Most importantly, it creates a positive, friendly feeling. It's flattering—we are impressed that the person

> **NUGGET**
>
> In Mexico, how you greet people can seem confusing. While their legal surname will include both their father's and mother's last names, when you address them you use only the paternal part of the surname. More importantly, do not use first names unless invited to.

POP QUIZ

You receive someone's card and the name reads Lee Tai-Wai David. Does this mean you should call him:

Lee? Mr. Tai-Wai? David? or Mr. Lee?

In Asia: Mr. Lee.

In North America: David or Mr. Lee.

has taken enough interest to remember our name. So become a name caller, in the best sense of the word.

You can't use someone's name if you are unsure of it. If the name is unusual or difficult to pronounce, ask the individual to repeat it. For example, Chinese people put their family name first, then follow this with their given names (usually two). Sometimes the given names contain a hyphen, sometimes not. This makes life interesting for Westerners, who are accustomed to the given name being placed first.

TOTAL ECLIPSE OF THE BRAIN

We have all been there: You see a person you know but can't remember his name. He greets you by name, and you just dive into a conversation, skirting the name thing, hoping for sudden recall. Your level of discomfort increases as you search the recesses of your mind.

The simplest solution is to "fess up" and tell him you are drawing a total blank. "Please tell me your name again?" Do this before you get too far into the conversation.

What about that unsettling experience of not remembering the name of someone you really should know? You can't

NUGGET

The *Three Times Ribbit* is a tip to help remember a person's name. Use the person's name three times. Say their name when you meet them and then find occasion to use it twice shortly thereafter.

This not only helps you remember their name; it will also help others who are part of the conversation.

say, "Please tell me your name again," especially if the reply would be, "What do you mean, boss? You can't remember my name?"

There is no elegant solution to this memory lapse. Your best bet is to leave the conversation before you get in too deep and find yourself having to introduce the person to someone else. Give a nice excuse and promise to return.

Sometimes, removing yourself from a stressful situation will help you remember. Or, go over to someone who may know the person's name. Then, reconnect with the person whose name you now know. Total eclipses of the brain happen to everyone—you are in good company.

GIVE A HELPING HAND

If you see someone struggling to recall your name (even someone you've met before), give that person a helping hand. Shake hands and introduce yourself by name. "I'm Darcy Rezac. We've met before. Nice to see you again."

Really good networkers always say, "Nice to see you," or "Great to see you." They know it works better than "Nice to meet you." The latter greeting is problematic when that person may respond, "We've met before."

> **NUGGET**
>
> If you are part of a couple, be careful not to use nicknames or pet names, such as "darling" or "honey," during networking events. If people are unsure of your partner's name and they don't have his or her card, your endearments are not helpful.

NAMETAGS TO THE RESCUE

When possible, use nametags at business and social engagements. Nametags work. They simplify the whole name thing.

If you are organizing an event, insist on them. If you have a guest list, preprint nametags and have them ready for your guests. We print our corporate logo on our nametags and color code for members and non-members.

NUGGET Avoid nametags with the expression, "Hello, my name is...." This is probably where nametags got the reputation as tacky. But, stick-on nametags are a good idea. Nametags with pins are not.

And yes, there is actually a right and wrong way to prepare a nametag. Print your first name large so it is easy to read. Your last name and company name can be written smaller, if space is limited. When people scrawl their names down quickly on nametags, it can resemble a doctor's prescription—impossible to decipher.

LOCATION, LOCATION

Yet more things can go wrong with a nametag, hard as it is to believe. At networking talks, when I discuss the correct placement of nametags, I start to hear strange hissing, ripping sounds. People are repositioning nametags to where they *should* be located: on the right-hand side of your chest, high enough to be easily visible. That way, when you extend your hand to shake a person's right hand, they have a direct visual line to your nametag. If the nametag is on the left-hand side, their eyes have to shift such that the two of you lose eye contact.

If you are wearing a conference-type nametag, the type on a string, prevent navel gazing; tighten the string so people aren't looking you in the stomach. A shoulder purse is not the place to attach your nametag. It's just not visible there.

NUGGET If you are wearing a clear name badge on a string, stash a few business cards in it, behind your name card.

ICE BREAKERS AND FIRE STARTERS

Though remembering names is important, it takes more than that to engage a person in conversation. You may need to start with a "ribbit" or two—small talk that revolves around topics such as sports or weather. It may not seem original, but sometimes the best way to break the ice is to talk about things you have in common. Weather is one of them—it's the "ribbit, ribbit" of humans. You know you've really overdone the small talk when you start talking about *The Farmers' Almanac.*

NUGGET

While in North America it is okay to talk about business from the get-go; in Japan, business is not discussed until the host has brought it up in conversation.

The ultimate goal is to take the conversation from ribbiting to riveting. In North America, an easy entrée is: "Tell me a little bit about what you do," or "What's the nature of your business?" The response should take the form of a *tribal introduction,* a mini version of a tribal story.

TRIBAL INTRODUCTIONS

A tribal introduction establishes your credentials and tells others what makes your company unique or interesting. It's short, sweet but memorable—twenty-one seconds or less. After hearing your tribal introduction, the other person should be intrigued enough to ask a follow-up question.

Boring version: "I'm in the coffee business. I work for Bean World. We sell coffee to grocery stores, restaurants and offices."

Tribal version: "I'm the personnel director of Bean World, the oldest gourmet coffee distributor in North America. We

POP QUIZ

What's your tribal introduction? Can you tell it in 21 seconds or less?

roast our beans right here on Marsh Street and employ two thousand local people. We were roasting coffee before Howard Schultz was out of diapers."

At least you now have something to work with, even if it is only, "Who is Howard Schultz?" (For you non-coffee drinkers, he's the founder of Starbucks.)

LITTLE STORY, BIG ANXIETY

A brief tribal introduction really comes in handy when you are in a group and the host says, "I'd like everyone to get up and tell us who they are and what they do." Sounds easy enough, doesn't it? But who hasn't felt a little anxious as their time arrives and the people ahead of you have introduced themselves in a brief, witty or confident manner that elicited laughs and smiles? In many ways, this is one of the toughest networking challenges. Round-robin introductions give you only a couple of seconds to present yourself, your company and your credentials, and there's peer pressure. Have your 21-second tribal introduction ready. Practice and preparation make anxiety evaporate.

LEGENDARY TRIBAL STORIES

If your introduction is an interesting one, it is likely to be repeated by others. From little tribal introductions can grow great tribal stories. Sometimes tribal stories become legends.

One of the most famous tribal stories, told in many Marketing 101 courses, concerns the Bata Shoe Company. Bata is one of the world's largest shoe manufacturers, selling over a million Bata-branded shoes every working day around the world.

In the 1950s, when Tom and Sonja Bata were expanding their company, they sent representatives to Africa to see if that region represented a market for their shoes. One Bata representative went down the west coast, and another down the east coast. Both sent telexes back to Bata's head office. One read, "No business opportunities here. No one wears shoes." The other stated, "Lots of business opportunities here. No one wears shoes."

This story has become legendary. When I asked Sonja Bata if it is true, she confirmed it is. She loves telling it.

While your company's story may not be on as global a scale as Bata's, it can still be interesting. Good stories get repeated again and again. You and your company become known by your tribal stories. That's personal and corporate branding at its most effective.

NUGGET

Disney employees have great tribal stories of their founder. All cast members at Disney venues tell stories about Walt that reflect the values of the organization and the man who started it.

TRIBAL STORY, NOT WAR STORY

What happens when you are in between tribal stories? You've been laid off and are out looking for a job, so what's your tribal story? "I was emptied out of the corporation in a bloody coup." This is not the right story.

Unfortunately, many people conducting a job search focus on the gory details. When networking for a new job, it's better to have a great tribal story of your previous company. Why not say, "I just spent five incredible years with Global Crossing as an IT specialist. It was an amazing learning experience, and now I am looking forward to applying my experience to a new opportunity." Tell a quick tribal story about yourself. Remember, you are a champion, not a victim.

KNOW WHAT'S GOING ON

While ribbiting may be a way to start a conversation, and tribal introductions make you memorable, after a minute or so, the conversation needs to develop substance. Either that, or the participants need to move on—and that's okay.

Know what's going on in your world—the whole world. Try to devote at least forty-five minutes a day to reading a wide range of local, national and international news. An incredibly efficient way to do this is on the web. Web sites like *The Paperboy* give you access to over 5,000 of the world's top newspapers and magazines. While you are having your morning coffee, you can read the very latest news from *South China Morning Post, The Guardian, Financial Times, International Herald Tribune* and *The New York Times,* or local news from most cities in the world. The worldwide web is one great network.

Equally important is to know what is going on in your own community. When you see someone, it's nice to be able to offer congratulations on a recent award, appointment, new contract or promotion. Or, when you first meet someone new, it's nice to be able to reply, "Yes, I know your company." Your local business magazines and the business section of the daily papers are a "must read" for positive conversationalists.

TABLEMATE TALK

Most networking situations allow people only a few minutes to make an impression. You chat and move on. In contrast, when you sit next to someone at an event for several hours, your conversational skills need to be sharper. Relax; you need not dive into business conversation right away.

Sometimes people want a break from the office. Avoid prickly points of conversation:

- politics and religion unless your views are similar
- kids, unless you both have them and want to talk about them
- intimate details of your personal life or theirs

Be engaging, be informed, be a good listener, ask good questions. If there are business opportunities, they will come because the two of you have hit it off.

ALICE

Treat people as equals and they happily engage in a conversation. Alice Mong, a well-connected networker who spent eleven years in Hong Kong, three of them representing the State of Ohio, shares her philosophy: "The bottom line is I enjoy people. They are not commodities to me. I hate it when people scope around and are quite mercenary. They drop you like a hot potato the minute they exchange business cards, check out your title or company and decide you are not worth their effort."

Alice's reaction is universal. Not treating everyone as equals has serious repercussions. We can all remember being snubbed or being someone's space filler. Be memorable for the right reasons.

THE FOURTH SECRET OF NETWORKING

« **Treat everyone as equals**. » It's a whole lot easier than trying to figure out who's who in the frog chain. Besides, it's the right thing to do.

The four Es are all about technique—establish, extend, exchange, engage. But, there is a "fifth" E. *Equality.* It has to do with attitude. Employ all five, and you'll stand out from the rest of the frogs. You are on your way to being a tree frog.

SUMMARY

the four E's— establish, extend, exchange, engage

Establish

- Establish eye contact and smile.
- Be focused.

Extend

- Be proactive. Be the first to extend your hand. Teach your kids to do the same.
- Develop a firm and confident handshake.
- Carry wet wipes and a hanky to keep your hands clean and dry.

Exchange

- Be the catalyst, the first to give out a card.
- Give cards to everyone in a group.
- If people don't give you a business card, ask for one.
- Exchange cards respectfully.
- Keep cards you are receiving in a separate pocket from those you are giving out.
- Your best card dispenser is your left hand.
- If you are the host of an event, encourage people to exchange cards.
- Cultural awareness is not a nicety; it is a necessity.

SUMMARY continued:

Engage

- If you don't understand or hear a person's name immediately, ask the person to repeat it.
- If people don't appear to remember your name, give them a break. Extend your hand and say your name.
- If you forget someone's name, "fess up" right away.
- Use a person's name throughout the conversation. To remember a name, use the Three Times Ribbit.
- Use nametags—they work.
- Wear nametags as high as possible, preferably on the right-hand side.
- Have your twenty-one-second tribal introduction ready.
- Ask questions based on a person's business card; give them one hundred percent of your attention.
- Devote forty-five minutes a day to reading a wide range of newspapers.
- It's okay to ribbit about the weather or sports to get a conversation going.

CHAPTER FIVE

travel in pairs

A Very Green Tag-Team

Once upon a time, there was an up-and-coming accountant frog named Polly who worked for McFly & Young. She was on the fast track to partner. She and her fiancé, Bob Wogg, went to her firm's annual Christmas party. Polly had butterflies in her stomach just looking out on that croaking sea of green. Polly took Bob's hand and moved into the chorus of frogs.

One of the partners at her firm came up to greet them enthusiastically. Polly panicked because she was drawing a total blank on his name. Bob stood patiently waiting for Polly to introduce him. Then Bob went and made things worse by saying, "Honey, why don't you introduce me to your colleague?" Polly was mortified. Actually, she almost croaked.

TRAVEL IN PAIRS

Travel in pairs just like the FBI. They know the value and importance of good back-up. When you travel in pairs, you have a sense of support and security. A skilled tag-teammate is your safety net in a crowd of perfect—and not-so-perfect—strangers. A tag-teammate doesn't have to be a spouse. This person can be a business associate, friend or family member. It is important that they understand they are part of a team. They are along to help, if needed.

There is great value in taking a teammate and not going it alone—particularly if you are just starting out. Here's how traveling in pairs can make for a positive experience:

- Tag-teammates introduce you to people they know you might be interested in meeting. Their network is working for you.

- Tag-teammates help you when you forget a person's name.

- Tag-teammates keep an eye out for each other. If one is trapped in a conversation or left high and dry, the other can come to their aid.

- Tag-teammates can sing your praises much better than you can. It's hard for you to launch into a story about yourself.

TAG-TEAMMATE DATING?

A tag-teammate doesn't have to be a person you know well. He or she can be an acquaintance, colleague, or someone you would like to know better, on a personal level.

Single career-oriented people often complain they never have time to meet anyone. A business-networking event is the perfect place to invite someone you aren't ready to invite for drinks or dinner. Find an event where you and your guest have a mutual interest; it could be a special speaker in town, a luncheon event or even a reception. It's about time you converted that sixty-hour-a-week job from a social millstone to an asset.

NUGGET

If the invitation says you and a guest, why not bring a guest?

ROMANCE HAPPENS

Peter C. Newman, of Zurich—author, columnist, political and business commentator—is probably best known for his definitive history of the oldest company in North America, the Hudson's Bay Company. Peter regularly works a trap line, just like the fur traders did, only his product is an incredible personal network.

I was invited to a reception one night by Peter's publisher to celebrate one of his new books. I couldn't make it, so I sent our top marketing consultant, Alvy, to represent The Board of Trade. She never came back. Peter married her. They lived happily ever after, and are one heck of a great tag-team.

NUGGET

"The Old Establishment was a club. The New Establishment is a network."

—From *The Wise Men* by Walter Isaacson and Evan Thomas, as quoted in Peter C. Newman's book, *Titans*.

THE STEP-FORWARD RESCUE

One of the simplest and most helpful things that your tag-teammate can do is help you out when you forget someone's name. Good tag-teammates know the signal: "When I don't introduce you, I'm not being rude. It's because I forgot the person's name, so here's how you can help me out. Just step forward, stick out your hand, introduce yourself and get their name for me." That is the Step-Forward Rescue.

CONE OF SILENCE

Good tag-teammates know where to sit when they attend a luncheon or dinner event. They don't always sit next to each other, but they are close enough to save each other from this dinner table predicament: One is talking to a person on his left. He momentarily turns his head to answer the waiter's question, "Whole wheat or white bun?", then turns back to his conversation mate only to find that person engrossed in a new conversation with someone else. He looks to his right, but all he sees is the person's back to him. There he sits in the *cone of silence.*

> **NUGGET**
> When sitting at a table, sit at least one seat away from your tag-teammate. That way, each of you will get to know two people but you will be close enough to help each other out.

His tag-teammate, sitting a couple of seats away, sees his dilemma and brings him into her conversation. See the importance of not being seated too close or too far away from a tag-teammate?

NOT ALL TAG-TEAMS ARE EQUAL

Not all tag-teammates are amusing or able to strike up a conversation with similar ease. Your tag-team partner may be a spouse who does not know many people at an event, a rookie networker or a friend who is shy. How can you help a "green" tag-teammate?

Prior to the event, read the invitation carefully and let your guest know the dress code. When you RSVP to the invitation, let the organizers know who your guest will be. This is particularly important if there will be preprinted nametags or a seating plan. It's bad form to arrive at an event that provides prepared nametags, with a guest who has to write his own with a felt-tipped pen.

Brief your teammate on some of the people he will be meeting. Example: "Doug Newton is the president of Terra Consulting, one of our largest clients. He's also a very big supporter of environmental causes. Mavis Brown is his second wife; she was formerly married to the CFO of the company." Now your tag-teammate has a fighting chance to remember names and avoid any foot-in-mouth conversations. But make sure he knows the Step-Forward Rescue, just in case your mind goes blank when you are making introductions.

ENCOURAGE INTRODUCTIONS

When tag-teammates don't work in the business world and may be uneasy about introducing themselves, encourage them to come up with their own personal tribal introduction. "I'm Lesley Rani, John's wife. John and I have three boys and I'm very active in the community's Science For Kids program." Remind them about the personal calling card idea.

WHEN TAG-TEAMS GO BAD

A smoothly running tag-team is a joy to behold, but tag-teams can go bad. We've all had the painful experience of being with a group in which one person can't be bothered engaging others in conversation and looks totally bored. If you are going to attend an event with someone, make sure you hold up your end of the tag-team bargain. Be an interested teammate.

Bad tag-teams spend entire networking events on the sidelines talking to each other. Why aren't they just at Starbucks having a latte together?

Then there are company cliques: colleagues who arrive at an event together and migrate en masse to the same table. Their boss did not have this in mind when he asked them to attend this event to *network* for the company.

J.J.

When tag-teams work well, the multiplier effect can be very powerful indeed. One of Gayle's and my most amazing experiences was landing aboard—then taking off from—an aircraft carrier at sea off the coast of San Diego. You hit the deck at 120 knots and come to a full stop in three seconds, or in launching, accelerate from 0 to 150 knots in 2.5 seconds!

While on board, we got to hang out with top-gun pilots and be a part of the whole amazing operation. The invitation to do this came out of the blue, one of the many random and unexpected things that have come our way as a result of networking.

When Gayle told J.J. Quinn, captain of the aircraft carrier (U.S.S. *Abraham Lincoln*), that she felt honored to be an invited spouse, J.J.'s response was, "We want our story told not ten times, but a thousand times."

The Navy invites opinion leaders from the business and the volunteer community to see what the Navy does and to tell the Navy's story. If J.J. invited only business and community leaders, and not their spouses, it would not be nearly as effective.

These couples take home the story of a lifetime and share it with absolutely everyone. If the spouse hadn't shared the experience, after the third or fourth retelling it would be, "Oh no, not the aircraft carrier story again." When a couple participates in such an experience together, they end up tripping over each other to tell the story. That's what the Navy wants: their story told not once or twice or ten times, but a thousand times.

OTHER TAG-TEAM POSSIBILITIES

"Take Your Kids to Work Day" is a springtime event that introduces children to the adult work environment. What about a "Take Your Kids to a Networking Event?" Every teenager and university student needs to acquire networking skills, yet at the hundreds of events I attend each year, I rarely see a networker with a university-age guest in tow.

At our organization, an innovative Leaders of Tomorrow program provides university students with first-hand experience networking with the business community. If your city or town doesn't offer such a program, think about introducing your children to networking. It's a skill they'll need regardless of career choice; in fact, networking skills will likely get them their first jobs. Who better than a parent to expose teens or young adults to the secrets of positive networking?

TWO PAIRS BECOME FOUR OF A KIND

David McLean, chairman of one of the largest railroads in North America, has had an incredibly active volunteer career. He has been everything from his sons' Boy Scout leader to the chairman of the national chamber of commerce. His wife Brenda has had an equally active business and volunteer career. When David was chair of The Board, his teenage sons, Jason and Sasha, came to our annual general meeting and to events in which their parents were involved. As teenagers, they even "subbed" when one of their parents could not attend. At an early age, Sasha and Jason learned to be interested listeners and respectful participants. They learned the skills of conversation and networking, but more than that, they experienced, first-hand, the importance of contributing to their community.

BE A NETWORKING MENTOR

Bring your teenage son who will graduate from university next year, or your daughter who can't decide if she wants to be a web developer or a veterinarian, along to an event. Get them feeling comfortable with operating in the adult world, and teach them what networking is really about. Buy them their first suit; trust them to pick something that's smart but cool. If they are searching for their first job, help them create their own business card. Start them on social events and as they get closer to looking for their first full-time job, be their mentor in networking for the best job.

> **NUGGET**
> If your spouse can't make an event, ask the organizer if you can bring your university-age son or daughter. Be the one to teach them how to network. You will be giving them a great advantage in life.

TRIP HORRIBILIS

A number of years ago, I took my daughter Sarah, nineteen at the time, to a conference at Oxford University. There were many social events and, since she had never been to England, I thought it was going to be a wonderful experience for her. She could see what dear old Dad does, and I could mentor her in the skills of networking, including a private gala dinner at magnificent Blenheim Palace.

On the way to the dinner, I told her about all the people she would meet that night, and about the history of the palace (where Winston Churchill was born in a cloakroom). After the main course in the grand ballroom, a lady dressed in a fancy gown and tiara sitting next to Sarah at her table—let's see, how can I put this politely—tossed her cookies.

Sarah was so unnerved, she stepped onto a balcony overlooking the gardens for some fresh air. Not realizing what had happened, I joined her to chat about how much I was enjoying the event. She looked at me strangely. Just then, a very inebriated professor weaving back and forth at the top of the stairs, tumbled down them like Humpty Dumpty, smacking his head on the pavement. After a moment, he stirred and crawled back up the steps, mumbling something about that person who must have hit him.

I don't know if Sarah would consider that event *networking*, but ever since then, when I dress for a fancy dinner, she looks at me with great sympathy. What she hasn't realized is that she's ready for anything in the world of networking.

FROG WISDOM

It's no secret that going as a tag-team can take the pressure off and make things more enjoyable, particularly if you are a networking novice. First Century B.C. Roman writer of mimes, Publilius Syrus understood this: « **An agreeable companion on a journey is as good as a carriage**. » Yes, the chariot is a nice idea, but teammate or no teammate, skill in working the pond makes networking more enjoyable, and that's what you are about to learn. Jump in.

SUMMARY

travel in pairs

- When the invitation says guests, bring someone. You'll have more fun. Remember to RSVP for them as well.
- Fill them in on the rules of being a tag-teammate.
- If your teammate doesn't introduce you to someone immediately, use the Step-Forward Rescue. Stick out your hand and introduce yourself. Now you've helped your teammate.
- Don't be afraid to sing the praises of your teammates. If they do great volunteer work or have won awards, it's better if you tell others about it.
- If your teammate doesn't have a business card, encourage him or her to get a personal card and develop a tribal introduction.
- Act as a host for your teammate.
- Use your teammate's name in conversation; everyone benefits from being reminded of names.
- Your tag-teammate doesn't have to be a spouse. Use an event as an opportunity to get to know a business associate better.

SUMMARY: continued

- Keep an eye on each other and come to the rescue, if one is trapped or left alone.
- Give your teammate a heads-up on the people you will be meeting.
- If you are a member of a tag-team, you have a responsibility to do your bit.
- Show your kids how to network; if you can, bring them as your teammate.
- If you are the organizer of an event, think about the value of inviting couples. Now two people will tell your story.

W

CHAPTER SIX

working the pond —positively

Fear of Ribbiting

Once upon a time there was a shy but very bright Western tree frog named Franklin A. Borealis. He was definitely "prince" material, but first he had to overcome some serious roadblocks. Just thinking about networking got Franklin jumpy.

So, he decided to join a fraternal association, the LOFLFM—Leaping Order for Frogs-Legs-Free-Menus, in hope of meeting some like-minded amphibians. He thought this would make for a softer landing in the networking pond.

It didn't take long for Franklin to start feeling more comfortable. He joined a committee lobbying fancy French restaurants to start serving chicken wings, and he even started introducing guest speakers.

Soon Franklin was ready to branch out to bigger, scarier ponds. He encouraged other fraternity brothers to test the waters with him. Soon, he had his own chorus of frogs who he saw at events. Franklin no longer felt like a flyweight.

WORKING THE POND—POSITIVELY

With or without a teammate, walking into a room full of strangers can be an intimidating experience. But to build a network, you have to meet a lot of new frogs. This can be particularly daunting if you are just starting out. Networking is not something often taught in business schools, or anywhere else.

> Every man loves what he is good at.
>
> —Thomas Shadwell, *A True Widow*
>
> NUGGET

Perhaps you haven't developed as large a circle of contacts as you would like, or you are among the *eighty percent* who haven't believed in networking—until now. Working a pond is about techniques anyone can learn. It just takes practice and a few simple skills. Armed with your positive networking mantra of discovering what you can do for others, you'll find it so much easier than you expected.

It starts by remembering that working the pond doesn't mean "strong-arming" people into talking with you, or collecting as many business cards as you can. Learning to circulate amongst your fellow frogs is a subtle skill; it's not a cannonball splash into the middle of the pond.

> You don't want to be a fly on the wall if you want to meet frogs.
>
> —Carol Fraser, Master tag-teammate
>
> NUGGET

TREADING WATER

Some of us frogs think we are networking when we're not. Chatting with a few fellow amphibians, introducing ourselves to one or two new pond dwellers, enjoying the free drinks and snacks, just doesn't cut it. This is just socializing, not networking. You want to circulate among the crowd to meet a wide variety of new frogs.

RAMOS

President Fidel Ramos of the Philippines is an extraordinary networker—one of the world's greats.

My organization hosted him as the guest speaker for a crowd of four hundred and fifty people. At the pre-luncheon reception for a hundred, President Ramos shook hands with everyone in the room. He looked each of them straight in the eye and greeted them with "great to see you," "how are you" or "glad to meet you." He then went back around and chatted with small groups. He literally touched everyone. When he left the room, the din of conversation was at least fifteen decibels higher.

His speech was a blockbuster. He got two standing ovations. Veteran ambassador John Trelevan, who has had postings in the Philippines and other parts of Asia, and has seen Ramos in action on many occasions, believes Ramos is the best networker he has ever met. "His secret is he is deliberate, focused and personal." These are three terrific networking qualities we can all emulate.

CIRCLES IN THE POND

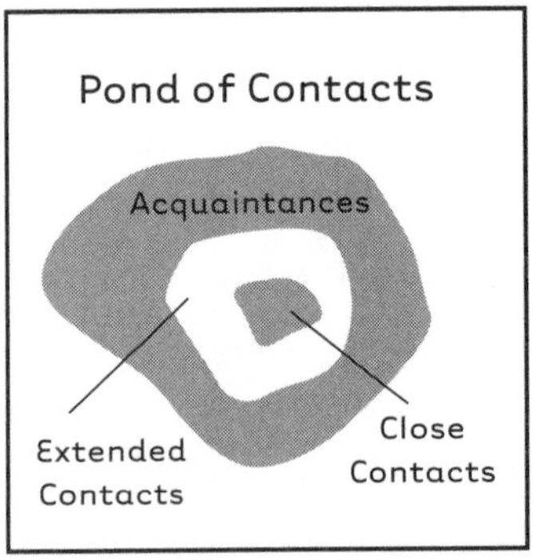

Networking events allow you to meet and develop contacts. They are where you begin to establish and grow your Pond of Contacts—your circle of *acquaintances, extended contacts* and *close contacts.* This is how you make your own small world even more powerful.

ACQUAINTANCES

Acquaintances are people you've met but may not know well. When you see them, you say "hi" and chat politely for a moment or two. That's about it. All of us have lots of acquaintances. Be careful not to dismiss their importance in your network, distant though they may be. Remember, the science of small worlds has proven just how powerful and significant even weak-linked contacts in distant networks can be.

EXTENDED CIRCLE

Your circle of extended contacts consists of business associates, colleagues or friends with whom you've formed a relationship, even if casual—something beyond just exchanging business cards. You've bonded at some level; you have a connection.

My circle of extended contacts probably includes three thousand people, or so. This is more than most because of the nature of my job and the length of time I have been at it. These are people that I would not hesitate to invite to an event or phone for advice. In return, I would expect them to call upon me from time to time. They do, and I am happy to help them if I can. Extended contacts can be hugely important in your life. Look after them.

CLOSE CIRCLE

Then there is your circle of close contacts. Close contacts are people who have proven to you, over time, that their focus is on what they can do for you or someone else. The two of you have either fought the "wars" together, developed strong bonds growing up together, or have just hit it off in some extraordinary way. Close contacts often become more than key business contacts; they can become very good friends.

My circle of close contacts probably numbers two or three hundred people. These are people with whom I speak "short-hand." I rely on them for sage advice and am always flattered when I can do something to help them. These people bring richness to my life. These are my princes and princesses.

BARB

It's all about technique when it comes to working the pond, and the results can be immediate. Barb Hislop, senior vice president of a Fortune 500 wood products company, found that out after attending my networking seminar one evening. A mere twelve hours later, at a power breakfast for women executives, Barb approached one of the first people she met and said, "I was told at my networking course last night that I should read your business card and ask you something about it." She glanced at the woman's card. "Tall Order Company, that's an interesting name. What does your company do?" The woman responded that it was a team-building company. Barb took her up on an invitation to try out her concept.

Imagine an Outward-Bound style cooking adventure on the edge of a wilderness lake. It was a bonding experience brought on by a high stress scenario, planned frustrations, deadlines, great wines and terrific food. It was not at all what Barb expected—it was better. She made some great new friends and business contacts, and she planned to put her managers through this program.

There are two great lessons here. Positive networking is a win-win activity and positive networking skills can be put into action immediately.

THE BIG SWEAT

Tell me, who hasn't had the following experience at least once in their business life? You arrive at a networking event, and as you look around, you see not a single familiar soul. If that isn't bad enough, everyone seems engaged in deep conversation—there's not even a straggler or two hanging around the edges of these groups. You wonder, "How am I supposed to nonchalantly break into one of these groups?" And how are you to know whether you are joining a chorus of frogs or a knot of toads?

So you sidle up to a group, and all conversation stops. Everyone turns and looks at you, the interloper. Or worse, you angle your way into a group and the conversation keeps flowing as if you don't exist. You feel like an eavesdropper.

BIG SWEAT MANAGEMENT

There's only one way to handle The Big Sweat situation. You need a crash course in confidence building. Public speaking programs such as Toastmasters and Dale Carnegie help you overcome your fear of crowds, large or small. You also get to work the pond among like-minded frogs. You'll become more comfortable striking up conversations with people in all sorts of situations, including breaking into a group.

Another way to build confidence is to join friendly "ponds" such as business, service or fraternal organizations. There you can meet people with whom you have mutual interests, and practice working a pond.

ARMED WITH ENTHUSIASM

The second way to attack The Big Sweat is to go to an event armed with enthusiasm. It's about attitude. If you don't want to be there, it will show. Although it may not have been in your job description when you were hired, networking is an essential business skill, and part of your job if you want to be successful. You can't get out of it, so get into it.

BE REALISTIC

Many people go to one networking event and expect immediate results. It just doesn't work that way. When people tell me, "I didn't meet anyone *worthwhile*," or "Nothing came from the contacts I made," I tell them that one event does not a networker make. Just showing up doesn't guarantee anything. It takes time to build relationships; don't expect otherwise.

The question you want to ask yourself is: What did my contacts gain from meeting me?

ACCEPT THE INEVITABLE

Many eighty-percenters avoid networking because of bad encounters. They happen to all of us; no one is immune. My own worst networking experience was a doozer. When just starting my job at The Board of Trade, I was invited to an event hosted by the stock exchange. I approached a high profile, somewhat flamboyant investment banker I had not yet met. I extended my hand and said, "Hello, I am Darcy Rezac. I am with The Board of Trade." He replied, "Good for you," turned and walked away. I was taken aback; it took me some time to come to grips with that put-down, until I learned Network Rule No. 7.

NETWORK RULE NO. 7

In their book, *The Art of Possibility,* Rosamund Stone Zander and Benjamin Zander have a chapter on their Rule No. 6. In a nutshell, it states: "Don't take yourself so damn seriously." In other words, lighten up. It is great advice. It was the inspiration for my Network Rule No. 7. And before you ask—no, there are no other rules.

When you encounter a networking setback, as all good networkers surely will, deal with it this way: *Get over it and move on.* This is Network Rule No. 7, and here's what I mean.

I came to understand that this investment banker had clearly decided that there was *nothing* I could ever do for him. That was his problem, not mine. Here was a person who had decided to move down the frog chain. Again, his decision, not mine.

Toads happen. You will have the misfortune of meeting them; my advice is to hop over them and move on.

CONFIDENCE: YOU CAN OWN IT

A great antidote to toad venom is confidence. To quote an old friend and amateur philosopher, Bill Frost, "You don't get what you want, you don't get what you deserve, you get what you get." You aren't Bill Gates or Julia Roberts, so don't beat yourself up for what you are not. You are who you are, and if you treat people right, you will be respected, liked and remembered. Have this attitude, and you can enter a room with confidence.

LOOK BEFORE YOU LEAP

Many people panic when they enter a room where they don't recognize a soul. There's a technique to make the situation easier: Stop, take a deep breath and look around. If you take the time to scan the room, you can "work the pond" logically. Figure out your best place to break into a crowd, and observe the group dynamics. You'll likely identify several choruses of frogs, perhaps a knot of toads and a few wallflowers.

Choose the path of least resistance and seek out a wallflower. This is a perfect opportunity to practice your new networking mantra: discovering what you can do for someone else. Put into practice the four Es: Walk over, extend your hand, introduce yourself and give out your card. Now you are in control of the situation, and can act more like a host than another wallflower.

After discovering some things about this person, do another gracious thing. Introduce him or her to other people you may now have recognized, or suggest that the two of you wander over and talk to some other people. Now you've just started a new group.

THE 28-SECOND HOVER

The hover is a more difficult maneuver, but it's an excellent way to meet new people. Walk up to a group of strangers and join them. Pick people whose body language indicates they are having a casual conversation—not a group apparently locked in a serious business discussion. Make sure you get in their line of sight. You have to get their attention to be able to enter their space.

Good networkers will stop their conversation and look at you. That is your

NUGGET

A social networking event is not the place to have a private business discussion. However, if you must have a few private words with someone, find a quiet place away from the crowd to do this, not in the middle of the action.

opening to leap right in and say, "Hi, I'm Pete Moss of Swampwater Beverages." Shake their hands and give them your card. The card is important in a situation like this, because if they were talking baseball scores, the focus may turn to business—their business and yours. Or you might have to join their conversation about how the Mariners and Red Sox did the night before.

The worst-case scenario is they don't include you. Hover for twenty-eight seconds, which is the maximum hover time most people can bear, then move on. Just remember the get-over-it maxim, Network Rule No. 7. They have decided you can't do anything for them.

START YOUR OWN GROUP

Starting your own group is a way to work the pond. Stand close to the entrance to the room, off to the side facing the doorway at an angle. This allows you to see people as they walk in. It puts you in a "greeting position." Forget hiding at the back of the room; that's networking Siberia—a cold and lonely place.

I often use this technique at networking events as a way to connect with known contacts. I make a point of getting to the event early; that way I don't have to hunt them down in the crowd. I stand near the front entrance where it is easy for me to catch their attention. We all know each other, and long ago learned the secret of discovering what we can do for one another. These are highly charged networks, and when we meet, a lot gets done in a very short time. There is also a lot of synergy created when extended contacts and acquaintances enter the room and join the group. It's like flies to flypaper.

BE THE HOST

A great way to create a group is to initiate introducing people to each other. Adopt the role of a gracious host, even if all you are doing is making introductions of people you have just met. "Franklin, meet Brooke. I've just met Brooke and she's an expert on greenhouse gases." It's not meant to usurp the role of the actual host; it's just a way—in your small group—to make sure everyone feels at ease.

THE GLOWING INTRODUCTION

I subscribe to the theory that you can sometimes create tribal stories for people just by the way you introduce them. I learned this from John Hansen, president of the Cruise Ship Association of the Pacific Northwest. He once introduced me to a colleague of his by saying, "I want you to meet Jim Cooney. He is the resident corporate philosopher of the Placer Dome mining company, and one of the most intelligent people you will ever meet."

Wow, that was some introduction, but John was right. Jim Cooney is brilliant. He speaks fluent Mandarin and reads Sanskrit and poetry in the original Greek. He has become a good friend and a source of much wisdom. John's introduction was worth repeating, and I always introduce Jim this same way. I don't know who gets more pleasure out of it, Jim or me.

INTRODUCTION IGNORED

The antithesis of the glowing introduction is the *introduction ignored.* A new person walks up to the group, and everyone just keeps on talking, ignoring the newcomer. It's that Eavesdropping 101 scenario from The Big Sweat, and it happens more frequently than it should.

Be a good networker and take the initiative. Politely stop the conversation as soon as you can by saying, "Hold that thought." Then, turn to the new person and introduce yourself to him or her, and begin the other introductions.

No one likes to feel invisible. Recap the conversation to that point and then let the person who was talking continue speaking.

A word of caution: It is rude to abruptly cut off the person who is talking, in your enthusiasm to engage the new person in the group. Look for an opening. This is why networking is an artful dance.

POND HOPPING

It takes finesse to leap from lily pad to lily pad without causing too many ripples, to carry on a short and pleasant conversation, then glide to another person or group. The goal is to become the Fred Astaire or Ginger Rogers of networking.

Whether you spend two or ten minutes with each new contact, give him or her one hundred percent of your attention. Think about the power of your personal network, and how your networks can connect.

NUGGET

Ginger Rogers did everything that Fred Astaire did. She just did it backwards and in high heels.

—Ann Richards, former Governor of Texas

- Do I know someone here who this person would like to meet?
- Do I have some information that would help this person in his endeavors?
- Would my product or service be of use to her?
- Would a follow-up be worthwhile?

That doesn't mean you have to find something nice to do for everyone you meet. You just need to be thinking about it.

POND HAZARDS

Working the pond means that you can sometimes get stuck in the weeds. Hazards include The Juggling Act and The Cling-on Factor.

Juggling a plate of hors d'oeuvres and a drink while shaking hands and giving out business cards is tricky stuff. A better solution: If you are hungry, make the time to go and eat. When you've finished eating, go network.

NUGGET

Networking and eating are mutually exclusive activities, except if you are sitting down.

The Cling-on Factor is when you meet someone and he or she "gloms" onto you. You can see that this person has decided to make you his or her best friend, even if just for one night. Cling-ons try to monopolize your time. You need to politely get "unstuck."

Here are a couple of options. Introduce this person to someone you know, and after a few minutes of conversation, graciously excuse yourself. If no one is available, politely say, "You will have to excuse me. There's someone I wanted to speak to and I need to look around the room for him. I will try and catch up with you later." This is not a particularly graceful solution, but if you've been an attentive listener, this exit will be acceptable.

A word of caution: Make sure that you aren't a Cling-on. Give people the option of moving on by saying, "It has been great talking with you, but I don't want to monopolize your time."

POND ETIQUETTE

Working the pond doesn't mean going only to events geared to networking, such as receptions, speeches and conventions. Parties, formal dinners, fancy galas, charity events and fundraisers are all great ways to work the pond.

NUGGET

When sitting at a large round table that has a tall sign with the table number, ask the waiter to remove it, once everyone has been seated. Now you have clear lines of vision across the table. It helps with the conversation flow.

Remember your pond etiquette. You must RSVP out of respect for the host. RSVP for your spouse or guest and confirm the spelling of his or her name. If you can't attend, do not send a substitute unless it has been cleared by the host.

WILL ANYBODY NOTICE?

People notice a no-show, so miss an event and you *might* be the topic of conversation. Events with half-empty tables scattered around the room force table guests to stare at empty place settings or at your lonely place card.

Once, when Gayle and I were at a fund-raising dinner in New York hosted by two well-known philanthropists, the hostess noticed that a couple hadn't shown up; there were six guests at a table set for eight. The hostess felt so badly about this that she made a point of joining the table from time to time, to ensure that everyone was having a good time. Later in the evening, when the master of ceremonies was thanking the hosts of the dinner, he commented on the hostess's gracious behavior towards this partially filled table. Now everyone knew that there were no-shows and wondered who they were. If they wanted to find out, of course, the nametags were still on the entrance table.

NUGGET

Have the waiter remove extra place settings as soon as you realize the people will not be showing up.

WHEN IT SAYS BLACK TIE

NUGGET

Never wear a light-colored suit to an evening event, unless it's your James Bond white dinner jacket.

Some ponds are splashier than others. When the invitation says "Black Tie" it means formal attire. Respect the host's wishes and dress accordingly. It's always better to be overdressed than underdressed. If you aren't dressed the part, you will feel like a frog out of water. And many will judge you as one of those just frogs. It's a lot harder to work the pond when you aren't feeling comfortable with your appearance.

NUGGET

The Basic Survival Kit

- 7 business cards
- Stain remover
- Hanky/Wet wipes
- Mints
- Needle and thread

When fancy events are sprung on you, here are some tricks. For men, the in-a-pinch "black tie" is a very dark plain suit, crisp white shirt, bow tie and dress shoes. For a woman, it's a suit that can make a "Superwoman" transformation from day to night by adding dress shoes and an evening bag. Now, all you need is a telephone booth.

YOU CAN ACT YOUR AGE

During the dotcom boom, chinos and logo-bearing polo shirts were signs you were one of the rich and famous. Now it's better to wear more business-like attire, to show you understand the concept of profitability. It doesn't mean you should dress like a fifty-year-old if you are only twenty-five. News flash: Casual Fridays are now on Saturday.

RECEIVING LINE DILEMMA

At more formal activities, you may encounter a receiving line. If you get in line and notice people in front of you telling their life story to the hosts—the backlog is growing and you wonder if you will ever get to the goodies—should you defect directly to the bar? No, it's important to let your hosts know you've attended.

When you finally get to the hosts, shake hands, introduce yourself, tell them who you represent and move on. Avoid a business pitch unless asked. However, if you are interested in talking with the hosts in more detail, tell them you would like to catch up with them later in the evening.

A receiving line can be a difficult place to hand out business cards. My advice: If you don't know the host, present your card.

POSITIVE VIBES

All of this working the pond takes a lot of time and seems like a heck of a lot of work. For many people, it also means leaving their comfort zone. But experienced networkers know that positive networking can actually energize. It becomes enjoyable as you get caught up in the rhythm of the network dance.

NUGGET

Networking feels like work when you start, but once you get into it, it really energizes you.

—Dan Muzyka, Commerce Dean

FITTING IT ALL IN

Working the pond has to be both enjoyable and efficient because today everyone is time-starved. Most networking events take place during precious hours reserved for family, friends and relaxing. Networking may mean getting up for a 7 a.m. breakfast meeting and not being able to say goodbye to your kids before they go to school, or not getting home until after they are asleep.

The questions you should ask yourself when you are working the pond include:

- Am I being efficient with my time?
- Am I spending my time in the right ponds?
- Is it worthwhile?

HENRY FORD: THE EFFICIENCY GUY

Henry Ford was the efficiency guru. He demonstrated—as those Model Ts rolled off the assembly line—that you can be more productive for the same effort. The term *productivity* is used to describe common measures of efficiency, such as miles per gallon, cost per unit, goals per game or, in the networking world, contacts per meeting.

We frogs must visit the right ponds and it's okay to measure our productivity. The best way to do that is to "count cards." It keeps you *honest*; otherwise you may get lulled into a false sense of security—"I'm here at an event, so I *must* be networking." Keep your *network shepa* high by having some guidelines for productivity.

The minimum number of cards that you should exchange at any event, big or small, is seven. If you make a personal commitment to exchange cards with seven people and have a quality conversation with each, you will be circulating the pond naturally.

I find that at a well-networked event I will exchange one to two dozen cards. That is probably a pretty efficient use of my time since I likely touch base with my close circle of contacts as well.

Friendly ponds such as chambers of commerce are some of the most efficient places to network. Here, the card-back ratio (the number of cards I get back for each given out) is highest. Of course, if I go to a social event, the card-back ratio will be much less than fifty percent, but it shouldn't be zero.

The key to productivity is to network among larger groups. For example: If you want to take someone to lunch, why not invite him to a luncheon with a speaker who would interest him? Lunch for two at a fancy French restaurant over frogs' legs and *Pouilly Fuisse* is really not as productive as inviting your guest to meet your network.

WHEN TWO BECOMES FIFTY-SIX

One of the best examples of productivity is turning two cards into fifty-six. If I am about to sit down at a table of eight at a networking event, I walk around the table and hand out my card to each of the seven other guests. Those who haven't handed out business cards start looking for them, and not only hand one to me, but also automatically give them out to the rest of the table.

Suddenly, fifty-six business cards have been exchanged. Everyone is connected, they know each other's names, where they work, what they do and how to contact each other. More output for less effort—Henry Ford would be proud.

NUGGET

When everyone is seated at the luncheon table, take a few minutes to organize the business cards you have received from your tablemates. Place them near you in the order that the guests are sitting around the table. This makes it easier to remember their names.

TEST THE pH OF YOUR PONDS

You want to know if you are working in *quality* ponds when you go out on your networking forays.

A busy architect friend who builds grand homes commented on the fact that he had little luck at networking. While he was very successful in his career, he said that there was no such thing as too much work, and he wanted to improve his networking—be more productive.

When I asked where he networked, he said he found time to participate in the association of architects and designers. "Wrong pond—those are your competitors," I told him. "You would be better off buying tickets to a gala charity event, where you will meet people who can use your talents."

NUGGET

pH is a measure of pond acidity. A pH of 7 is in perfect balance, not too acidic or too alkaline. When ponds go toxic, as they sometimes do, it is time to leave the party. Or drain the swamp. Your call.

It worked. He has added new clients, and his tuxedo is getting quite the workout. Look for quality ponds and test their pond pH—are they working for you? Quality ponds are different for each individual.

LEON WALRAS: THE ECONOMIC UTILITY GUY

You have been putting in lots of hours working the pond, but as Peggy Lee sings: *Is that all there is?* Is it really worthwhile?

Here's where the concept of *utility* comes in. The great Swiss-French economist, Leon Walras, developed the general equilibrium theory, a fancy way of saying that people will continue to buy, or do something, if it is useful—if it continues to have some *utility*. Common measures are rates of return on investments or interest rates.

Utility is something only you can evaluate. Because all of us are time-starved, we need to assess how we use our networking opportunities. How *useful* is networking the way we presently do it? It is wise to assess your technique and your ponds from time to time. Ask these questions:

- Are you in the right ponds?
- Are your contacts benefiting from your being there?

- Is what you are doing contributing to your life, your personal and professional happiness?

At the end of the day you ask yourself, is the effort worthwhile? You bet it is. When we work the pond well, our networks become connected to other networks and it becomes a small world. Leon Walras would have been dazzled by the utility of it all.

FROG WISDOM

A wise old frog once wrote, « **You can't do anything about the length of your life, but you can do something about the depth and breadth of it.** » At the end of the day, positive networking is all about building valued relationships. So, working the pond is not really "work."

SUMMARY

working the pond—positively

- Approach working the pond by thinking about what you can do for someone else.
- Join Toastmasters International or Dale Carnegie as a way of building your confidence fast.
- The pond is one of the more effective places to keep all your contacts—acquaintances, extended and close—warm. It's also where you develop new contacts.
- When you enter a room of strangers, stop and take your time. Look around for the best opportunities: friendly groups, wallflowers or acquaintances.
- Take on a host mentality. Introduce people as soon as they enter your group. Be gracious to everyone.
- Don't let anyone do the twenty-eight-second hover around you; your positive networking manners are better than that.
- You'll probably experience rejection; get over it. When in Toad country, move on. Remember Network Rule No. 7.

- Standing up, eating, drinking and networking all at the same time is too much multi-tasking for anyone.

- The front of the room is the place to meet people or start a group. Avoid the back of the room—networking Siberia.

- Don't judge a book by its cover; you'll be surprised who you meet.

- Introduce people with a flattering introduction whenever possible.

- You will feel more at ease if you follow the pond etiquette rules.

- Your time is valuable. Make sure you are in the right pond and using your time efficiently.

- Set a goal of meeting seven new people and exchanging cards, at any event. This will keep you circulating, not stuck in the mud.

CHAPTER SEVEN

opportunity is everywhere

Grandstand Ralph

Once upon a time there was a young doctor frog named Ralph Rani. He was a dermatologist and was attending his first large medical conference. He wanted to make a big splash amongst his peers and the more experienced frogologists. At the end of the session entitled "Results of Clinical Trials on Wart Removers," Dr. Ralph stood up and asked a question.

He thought that this was his opportunity to let everyone in the room know that he was an expert on the subject. Puffing himself up, he prefaced his question with much croaking and ribbiting. When he finally got to his question, he made it a three-part question. The rest of the frog docs just rolled their big bug eyes. They were no longer interested in the wart removal trials; they just wanted something that would remove Dr. Ralph.

OPPORTUNITY IS EVERYWHERE

Networking opportunities are everywhere. It's just a matter of knowing the right way to:

- meet more people and expand our networks
- make the most of these opportunities
- turn a mistake into an opportunity
- recognize and seize great opportunities right in front of us

SILVER PLATTER ORGANIZATIONS

The easiest places to start expanding your network are your local chambers and boards of trade. These are organizations based on the concept of business networking. They are a great place to practice your networking skills because they give you "permission to network."

The great thing about these permission-to-network organizations is they have already done most of the work for you. These are opportunities served up on a silver platter. They bring groups of people together for a reception, conference, meeting or party. Someone else has organized the event; you just have to show up with your business cards.

NUGGET

Over 100,000 business cards are exchanged at The Board of Trade annually. That's permission to network.

A CLEAN SHEET OF PAPER

When Judy moved to Hong Kong to become director of administration and human resources for an international firm with seven hundred employees, she was starting with a clean sheet of paper. She had a seventy-hour-a-week

NUGGET

Local business organizations are the place to start, but for greater reach, consider joining their national counterparts as well, such as the U.S. Chamber of Commerce.

job, in a new country with new colleagues. She did not want to be stuck in her office all the time, so she joined the American Chamber of Commerce. Not only did she attend speaker luncheons, she became a member of one of the Chamber's working committees. "It was a completely painless way to break into a new community. I was fast-tracked into a group of new contacts." Through all this, she met a cross-section of business people, politicians and business visitors from different countries.

NUGGET

Steve Olson, policy chief at the Pacific Basin Economic Council in Honolulu, agrees that *network shepa* is probably highest in Hong Kong. "It is amazing to attend a luncheon at the Hong Kong General Chamber of Commerce. Business cards literally dance around the table and people get right down to business. I call it *turbo-networking*."

JOIN UP

Other organizations that provide opportunities and give "permission to network" are large international associations such as the Rotary Club, Kiwanis and Lions Club. Local breakfast clubs are often tourism- or marketing-based organizations. Women have their own networking associations, often tied to a particular industry. All typically offer a wide range of interesting speaker luncheons, networking sessions, golf tournaments and other social activities. Local newspapers and business magazines carry frequently updated lists of upcoming talks, seminars or activities. See what is available in your area and start meeting some new people.

NUGGET

If you belong to a Rotary Club, you can go to a Rotary meeting anywhere in the world.

NETWORKING BY ASSOCIATION

One of the best memberships is an associate membership, which grants access to a group where you qualify as a service provider to members. For example, franchise lawyers can become associate members of the International Franchise Association. They attend franchise conferences, which give them an opportunity to meet franchisors and franchisees—exactly their market.

POP QUIZ

How many organizations do you belong to?

What four key organizations could you join?

OPPORTUNITIES IN DISGUISE

While permission-to-network events are great ways to meet people, many potential networking opportunities don't come with a heads-up stating, "This is a networking event." Charity fun runs, receptions organized by a company to launch a new product, a church picnic—all represent valuable networking opportunities.

PARTICIPATE AND CONTRIBUTE

Getting involved in any group activity provides new networking opportunities. Work on a political campaign or buy a ticket to a fundraising dinner. You've got something in common: you support the candidate.

If your passion is the arts, music or amateur sports, volunteer to help at upcoming events—the jazz festival, film festival or that 10K bike race. Local newspapers often include notices from organizations looking for volunteers. Type the word "volunteer" and your city name into an Internet search engine to find volunteer associations in your area, then discover what you can do for someone else. Pick something for which you have a passion, so you will stick with it.

Charitable organizations ranging from children's hospitals to the United Way require volunteers, and you can meet interesting people as you serve up hot dogs and hamburgers or answer pledge lines at the local telethon.

FREE SPEECH OPPORTUNITIES

Your opportunity to make new contacts could come from giving away some expertise for free. Most of us have skills or knowledge that we can impart to others. If you are a lawyer, give a talk to the photography association on partnership agreements. If you are a photographer, give a talk on digital photography to a tourism association. Use those Toastmasters or Dale Carnegie skills; they are perishable. Frogs further up the frog chain use this method to find new opportunities.

If you aren't keen on giving a speech, why not write an article for your industry association magazine? Invest in a black and white headshot. Most publications are happy to receive a professional photo to accompany the article. Becoming recognized as an expert helps you become better known for the right reasons.

SPEAK UP

Opportunity often has nothing to do with networking events, conferences or business get-togethers. The opportunity to build your network can come over a chat with another parent at the early-morning peewee hockey practice, or through finally introducing yourself to that person you see in the elevator every morning. It's the difference between saying nothing and being the one to start a conversation. Opportunities reveal themselves when you start conversations.

AIRPLANE DILEMMA

Airplanes would seem like a great opportunity to network, but there is something about such close proximity over an extended period of time that makes networking on airplanes a little dicey.

You get on an airplane, find your seat and stow your carry-on luggage. Should you start a conversation with your seatmate, or do you really want to enjoy those two, five, ten hours of sweet solitude?

When you sit down, introduce yourself and say a few words to your seatmate. Respect each other's space. If there is a meal during your flight, that's a good time to socialize. You just never know what you might learn at 35,000 feet.

CAN I HAVE YOUR AUTOGRAPH?

On a flight from Hong Kong to Kuala Lumpur, I exchanged a few pleasantries with the chap in the next seat, but he seemed deeply engrossed in a thick book. It was not until the meal arrived that we started chatting. It turned out he was a mining engineer on his way to a project in Myanmar, and he had grown up in my hometown. I gave him my business card and his eyes lit up.

"This is absolutely incredible," he said, "but I've just read about you in this book." He showed me the cover of the book, Peter Newman's *Titans.* I couldn't believe it. What were the chances of this happening?

What's more amazing about this "perfect timing story" is that Newman's book carries only few lines about me in its seven hundred pages. Had this man and I not bothered to introduce ourselves, we would never have had this "small-world" experience.

To this day, we probably both tell the story. You never know what can happen until you start talking.

A MISTAKE MAKES AN OPPORTUNITY

Sometimes a mistake we make opens the door to an opportunity. A fine gentleman and one of my favorite people, Joe Segal, lunches every day at the Four Seasons Hotel. Like clockwork, he arrives every day at noon. Joe has his own table.

Frank Borowicz, a lawyer with princely networking skills, was meeting with colleagues. His group included *another* Mr. Segal, who had booked a table for lunch at the same restaurant. Frank, the first to arrive, told the maitre d' he was meeting Mr. Segal. Frank was seated at Joe's table—the *wrong* Mr. Segal's table—and was soon joined by his colleagues.

Out of character, the punctual Joe Segal arrived late. Unamused to see a group of lawyers eating, drinking and making merry at his table, he walked over and let them know they were at *his* table. Frank and his group, being in the middle of their meal, couldn't easily pack up and change tables. However, they did beat a relatively hasty retreat, and Frank returned to his office feeling bad about the mix-up.

Since Frank is a proponent of the theory, "It's not the mistake, it's the recovery that counts," he phoned Joe. "Joe, I want to take you to lunch." There was a long pause and Frank continued the sentence, "at *your* table." It was the beginning of a wonderful friendship.

NUGGET It's not the mistake that matters; it's the recovery.

OPPORTUNITIES THAT YOU CREATE

As you gather your circle of contacts, you'll probably be invited to events as someone's guest, but why wait for an opportunity to land in your lap? Purchase a ticket to any number of great networking opportunities. Support a local fundraiser or gala for a worthy cause by buying two tickets for you and your tag-teammate. If you or your company have a budget to invite others, do so. Purchasing a table at an event allows you to choose an interesting mix of people, all with the potential to help each other. If your company does not have the budget to host a table, contact some acquaintances and see if you can put a table together.

SEEKERS AND PURVEYORS OF KNOWLEDGE

You can also create networking events of your own, but there are some secrets to doing it right. Rich content, a thoughtful mix of people and interesting venues enhance any networking event. That's how the great networkers do it.

I have had the pleasure of seeing three of the world's great networkers in action. They take on a catalytic role of bringing people together and facilitating their active participation in the exchange of knowledge. They ask thought-provoking questions and want everyone to express their views and share them. They are consummate listeners.

NO PASSENGERS ON THIS BOAT

Entrepreneur and owner of *Ripley's Believe It or Not!,* Jimmy Pattison does this with guests on his boat. Actually, it's a yacht, but Jimmy's the kind of guy who just calls it a boat. He asks everyone to speak briefly on something that they "really care about," and he means everyone. If couples attend, he invites them both to speak. On Jimmy's boat, there are no "passengers."

CLEAR THINKERS REQUIRED

Tom Donohue, president and CEO of the three-million-member strong U.S. Chamber of Commerce, organizes very popular small dinners and invites a wide variety of guests. The express purpose is the exchange of ideas. Tom brings together twenty titans of industry and empowers each with just one minute to talk on a key issue. Then Tom makes his summation. He connects all the dots in a masterful fashion, tying together what everyone has said. Chamber board member Barry Appleton says, "It is this distilled knowledge of clear and concise thinking that is the magic that keeps everyone coming back for more."

CATALYTIC QUESTIONS

Klaus Schwab, founder of the World Economic Forum, may be best known for standing on the world stage and asking profound questions about the state of the world of U.K. Prime Minister Tony Blair, the President of the United States, Shimon Peres or Michael Dell. What's interesting is that Professor Schwab does the same in private situations, off the world stage.

At a small casual dinner, he and his wife Hilde stimulate conversation on global issues. They pose a thought-provoking question such as, "What do you see as the biggest challenge facing the world today?" The expectation is that every one of the guests provides their view—they make everyone an active participant. Amazing energy fills a room when people are asked for their views. And everyone there gets to benefit from everyone else's answers. These great networkers are not only seekers of knowledge; they are catalysts in the exchange of ideas.

NO YACHTS OR PRIME MINISTERS?

While most of us don't have prime ministers and Fortune 500 business gurus at our beck and call, or yachts and the world stage at our disposal, that doesn't mean we can't learn from great networkers. You can create more opportunities for everyone if you bring a good mix of people together in an interesting venue and ask stimulating questions to raise the level of dialogue.

THINK OUTSIDE THE BOARDROOM

You can do some simple, inexpensive networking events in-house. Invite a group of people to your office for a breakfast meeting, lunch or after-work event. Think of some interesting venues at which to hold an event—a factory floor, perhaps. People are curious to see interesting operations. I've been to a dinner party in the kitchen at the Hyatt hotel and to business events in aircraft maintenance hangers with a real 747 as the centerpiece instead of an ice sculpture. Think outside the boardroom.

With a little imagination and flair, you can create a reason for people to come to your event. It could be a wine tasting with a wine expert in your meeting room, a get-together to watch a televised local government budget presentation (provide report cards to grade the budget), or a reception introducing a business associate from another part of your organization. Who could you invite as a "guest of honor" to an in-house event?

TELL IT LIKE IT IS

When sending out the invitation, tell it like it is: *Bring business cards; this is a networking event.* Have nametags prepared. Ask for each guest's approval to create a list of names and email addresses of attendees. Then provide that contact list of all attendees the day after the event. You are moving up the frog chain.

NETWORKERS R US

Networking opportunities are not just external. How many managers tell their staff, "Go out to the event and really use the networking skills that we've taught you?" In many businesses, networking is a word people love to hate. They will go out of their way to call it something else: meet-and-greet, get-to-know or make-some-contacts.

As a manager, you are missing out on a cost-effective marketing tool if your staff do not know the secrets of positive networking. Train them to network and provide opportunities to use these newfound skills. Even seasoned business people need a little reminder of networking opportunities and pitfalls.

Send your people to business events in the community, host tables at luncheons and invite guests or create in-house networking opportunities where your staff can practice networking skills. Send them in tag-teams, then follow up with them. Find out whom they met and what they discovered about these people. Build a team networking spirit.

Although companies tend to focus on

NUGGET

Checklist for Hosting Events

- tell people it's a networking event.
- remind them to bring cards.
- give them nametags.
- send out a list of participants after the event with your follow-up note.

networking opportunities outside their organization, discovering what you can do for someone else is just as good an idea inside your own organization. Have an intranet bulletin board where all employees can post client names and potential sales opportunities so everyone can access each other's network of contacts. Let them know that every link, no matter how weak, is important. That weak link might lead to the close contact needed. Now your company is working with a network of networks.

POP QUIZ

Does your company have a mission of networking excellence? Do your staff know that networking is part of their job? Do all your staff have business cards and understand their importance?

DO IT YOURSELF

If you aren't in a position to effect these kinds of changes yourself, you can still have an impact. Every company is interested in ways to build its business, so suggest ways to build a company that knows how to network. Why wait for your company to send you to networking events? Buy your own ticket and go.

GATEKEEPERS AND CROCODILES

Opportunities are missed when people set up gatekeepers. This could be an assistant who screens calls and emails, or a receptionist who doesn't pass on messages. There are also those who serve as their own gatekeepers—people who don't return phone calls. These are frogs that think they need a crocodile guarding their moat. In most cases, it's overkill. Few people are so important that they can't answer their own calls.

DOOR OPENERS

Billionaire Jimmy Pattison's executive assistant, Maureen Chant, is the opposite of a gatekeeper. She is a door opener. People always tell me (and they seem incredulous), "I called Jimmy, and Maureen put me right through," or "I called Jimmy, and Maureen told me he'd get back to me—and he did."

Jimmy is one of North America's most successful entrepreneurs because he's open to opportunities, and Maureen knows it.

THE CEO QUOTIENT

A sign adjacent to the parkade elevator in the building where I work reads, "Remember your level." It's good advice, because in my experience, too many people only want to "network up." They don't believe that a networking event is worthwhile unless there is a strong contingent of CEOs and senior management, even though they themselves are mid-level managers. They think networking is about rubbing shoulders with the bigwigs.

That is not always the case. In fact, it's good to remember your level. Peers are some of our most important networking contacts. If we meet another mid-level marketing manager and establish a long-term relationship, that person may eventually become the vice president of marketing. Even princes and princesses were all frogs once.

Of course, this doesn't mean you shouldn't seek out events geared to "higher ups." Just don't assess a networking event's worthiness based on the CEO quotient.

WHO, ME?

At the other end of the spectrum are those who are too aware of their level, people who don't think they should go over and speak to the CEO or guest speaker.

At speaker luncheons, before everyone sits down to lunch, I will often look around for someone I think would like to meet the speaker (who might be a political or business leader).

Sometimes their initial reactions surprise me. People say, "Who, me?" or appear to be thinking, "Why would that person want to meet me?" My answer is: why not? Treat all people as equals—including yourself.

THE EARLY FROG GETS THE FLIES

Going to an event and just hoping you will meet some interesting people is not the best way to maximize an opportunity. If there is someone you want to meet, you need to be bold. Seize the opportunity and simply introduce yourself to that person. Let him know why you wanted to meet him and have a meaningful conversation, even if it is short.

If there is an empty seat next to the person you want to meet, why not sit there? Sitting at the same luncheon or dinner table is one of the best ways to get to know someone. During the meal, you have the opportunity to spend time together. If the table is not reserved, simply walk up and ask if you may join the person. Introduce yourself, sit down and begin a conversation.

Even with prearranged seating, if there are people you want to meet, find out where they are sitting. Check the seating plan and nametags on the table at the entrance to the event. During a break in the meal service or between speeches, people usually stand and chat briefly with one another. Use this opportunity to say hello, because when the event is over, people disperse quickly.

In order to seize all these opportunities, you can't be a laggard. Arrive early so you can locate people or sit where you want. Too many people arrive just in time for the lunch and miss the reception. They miss some great networking opportunities. Remember, the early frog gets the flies.

FROG CLUSTERS

Opportunities are missed when we stay with the group. I see it all the time—frogs who come to networking events and conferences, and then sit in a tight little knot during dinner. Sometimes you'll find a chorus of them ribbiting around a table of hors d'oeuvres, or standing in a huddle catching up on office events. Why bother taking two hours, or worse yet, two days, away from the office to go somewhere with amazing networking opportunities, and then spend most of the time with people you know?

NOT ROCKET SCIENCE

Business school dean Dan Muzyka, who started his career as a real rocket scientist, is one of the savviest networking deans I know. He is so into networking that even his dog, Charbon, wears a nametag at Dan's annual summer garden party.

Dan and I were on a high-profile trade mission to Hong Kong with a group of business people and government officials. Each member of our group had committed nearly a full day in flying time and then lost a day thanks to the International Date Line. They had also incurred considerable expense to be a part of this very high-level international meeting.

After arriving at our hotel, we went to the reception our trade mission organizers were hosting prior to the opening dinner that night. This reception was our group's briefing prior to the start of the conference. As time drew closer to the opening dinner, someone piped up and said: "Let's go downstairs early so that we can get a table and all sit together."

Dan couldn't believe his ears. "Time out, time out," he said, waving his hands. "We didn't come all the way to Hong Kong to talk to each other. Let's spread out and sit with different people."

I don't know if Dan uses this as a case study on "how not to network," but it would have been a failing grade performance in his class. Remember Dan's advice: spread out.

NUGGET

When with a group of business associates at an out-of-town conference, make a point of having everyone bring new people they've met to social get-togethers after the day's events. You can go bowling with your office mates when you get home.

THE POWER OF QUESTIONS

One of the most powerful ways to meet new people is to ask a question in front of a large group. You have a golden opportunity to introduce yourself, not to one, two or seven people, but to hundreds.

I first recognized this power of asking questions during a session at a conference in Singapore. Before a group of six hundred people, I stood up during the "Q&A" session to ask a question of the prime minister. I introduced myself—my name, organization and country—and asked my question.

Later, at the day's luncheon, as I walked around the table and introduced myself ("I'm Darcy Rezac"), to my surprise, many people answered: "Yes, I know." Several said they remembered me from the question session earlier. In the corridor, people nodded to me in recognition. What I realized is that when I stood up to ask that question, I introduced myself to six hundred people.

JULIE

After I told this story at one of my networking seminars, a young woman in the audience decided to put it to the test herself at a function featuring the Winter 2010 Olympic Bid Committee. At the end of a presentation that drew two hundred and sixty attendees, the young lady from my networking class stood up and took the microphone. "My name is Julie Connolly, marketing manager for the Commodore Ballroom. I would like to know what a small business like the Commodore Ballroom can do to assist in the Olympic bid."

All four panelists responded to her question, each reinforcing the name of the Commodore Ballroom, a dance hall and entertainment facility. Not only did she dazzle her boss with the branding and recognition her simple question generated, but the Commodore ended up booking a major community awards event as a direct result of that encounter. You can't buy advertising like that.

So step outside your comfort zone, as Julie did. She got it and discovered the power of asking a question.

NUGGET

If you've read up on the speaker, you can ask an interesting question that relates to your background knowledge and her just-finished speech or comments.

LINE OF SIGHT

There's more to "the question" than simply standing up and asking it. Where you sit is key. Sit in the front corner away from the podium so you are close enough for the speaker to see you and recognize your face. This is important if you want to speak with him or her after the session. Turn towards the speaker to ask your question. In this position, most people in the room will also be able to see your face. It's a much better idea than sitting in the middle of the room, where half of the attendees will see only your back and the others have to turn around to see you.

BE THE FIRST

Try to be one of the first hands up to ask a question. Most people are reluctant, but think of it this way—you are helping out the speaker. Who hasn't heard the emcee ask, "Any questions?," only to be greeted by dead silence? Everyone will be relieved when you ask your question and it will usually cause others to follow your lead and ask one as well.

YOU HAVE 28 SECONDS

You now have 28 seconds to introduce yourself and ask a question. "Why 28 seconds?" people ask. "Because 30 seconds is too long. At 30 seconds, people start looking at their watches. At 40 seconds, they start *shaking* them."

Use this short time wisely. Stand up, introduce yourself by name, title and company—not only because this is a branding opportunity for you and your firm, but to enlighten the audience and the speaker. It may help them better understand your question.

NUGGET

Run along sonny, you are beginning to bore me.

—Mae West

Remarkably, most people don't consider this important technique when they get up to speak in front of a crowd—whether it is to ask a question or give an opinion. Remember your *network shepa*; be aware of the opportunity to introduce yourself to others.

BE HEARD

Too many people don't speak up when they ask their question. If there's a microphone, wait for it. If the speaker or emcee is not experienced on the podium, he may not repeat the question. Now there's a problem. People turn to each other and whisper, "What was the question?" If people haven't heard the question, who really cares about the answer?

GET THE HOOK, PLEASE!

Every speaker's second-worst fear is when someone prefaces his question with this remark: "I have a *three-part* question for the speaker." Make your question straightforward—a one-part question, succinct and to the point. It's embarrassing when a speaker looks to the emcee or other panelists as if to say, "What is that person asking?"

Every speaker's *number-one* fear is the person who prefaces her question with this remark: "I'd like to make a comment before I ask my question." This is not your personal soapbox. It may be fair game to compliment the speaker: "I found your theory on …very enlightening, and my question is…" If your question is going to be controversial, a preface with a

NUGGET

Throwing the speaker a puffball question just for the sake of asking a question is a waste of a good question. Ask a question that will be interesting for most people in the audience.

compliment may prevent you from being tagged "hostile questioner."

MAKE IT INTERESTING FOR ALL

There are always people who ask questions with no relevance to the topic; they use question periods as an excuse to hear their own voices. Here's the rule of thumb: Your question should be sufficiently interesting that others in the audience will care about the answer. Think about your question during the speech. Write it down; I even recommend you read it out loud if you aren't comfortable winging it.

It's easier for me to say you should do this than it is for you to do it if you do not have a lot of experience. Professional public-speaking courses are the best way to gain confidence. The best way to boost your comfort level is to stand up frequently and ask concise, intelligent questions.

NUGGET

When attending international conferences, state your country as part of your introduction.

THE SOCRATIC FROG?

The Socratic method demonstrates the power of asking questions. Twenty-five hundred years after the great philosopher, Socrates, walked the hills of Athens, his teachings are in the midst of a revival. Complete college courses are being taught using the modern variant of the Socratic method of learning.

Ronald Gross's book, *Socrates' Way: Seven Master Keys to Using Your Mind to the Utmost*, lays out these keys: "Know thyself, ask great questions, think for yourself, challenge convention, grow with friends, speak the truth, strengthen your soul." These basics still apply. Questions are powerful when done well. Just ask the reporters of *60 Minutes*.

Socrates would likely feel right at home in the kingdom of *The Frog and Prince.* The philosopher's friends thought he looked like a frog, with his "protruding forehead, bulging eyes, squashed nose, bulbous lips, head set without any neck," according to Gross. No doubt he was an *Amphibius rex.*

FROM RIBBITING TO RESULTS

The most powerful part of recognizing and maximizing an opportunity is seeing a situation with great potential, then doing something with it that truly makes a difference.

Peter Fraser and Jay Rockey, both of Seattle, are consummate networkers. A few years ago The Rockey Company, one of the leading public relations firms in the country, staged a networking event to promote better business connections between corporate leaders in Seattle and Vancouver. Peter and Jay had invited three-dozen ranking CEOs from these two cities to a luncheon at the consul general's home in Seattle.

The Canadians, quite appropriately, arrived by Beaver floatplane, landing in front of the magnificent diplomatic residence, across the lake from Bill Gates' home. After a wonderful meal the group was chatting amicably. It was a pond of happy frogs who thought they were princes. But it was just a "ribbiting" experience.

That was the problem. No one got beyond ribbiting. As Peter and Jay wandered about, they realized that nothing of substance was being discussed. So as the event was winding up, Peter took the microphone and said, "It has been great getting to know each other, but is there something—just one thing—we can do together to make this event truly worthwhile?"

After a pause, someone suggested, "Border delays are a huge hassle for business travelers. Why don't we work together to do something about it?"

The group agreed, on the spot, that a task force be established to lobby both governments for better border access for business. The result—a year later—was a pilot project, the first fast lane between Canada and the U.S., which allowed pre-screened travelers through faster. The program was eventually implemented coast to coast, and brought hundreds of millions of dollars in additional business between the two largest trading partners in the history of the world. Just one opportunity—one question—triggered it all.

THE FIFTH & SIXTH SECRETS OF NETWORKING

The fifth secret of positive networking is: « **Give everyone the password to the network: permission**. » Give yourself and everyone you come in contact with permission to network. Be open to new people and let them into your network. The multiplier effect can be astonishing.

While the fifth secret of networking is about attitude, the sixth secret of positive networking is about a simple technique: « **Learn the power of asking questions and use it.** » This is a very powerful tool in both group settings and one-on-one conversations. It often means stepping outside your comfort zone. Be bold. Most people don't do it; be someone who does. Socrates was famous for it.

SUMMARY

opportunity is everywhere

- Opportunities to expand your network are everywhere. Recognize them, maximize them or create your own.
- To develop opportunities, you need to meet and talk with more people in both social and business situations.
- Join organizations and participate in them: local chambers of commerce, boards of trade, Kiwanis, Rotary, Lions Clubs, industry-specific organizations, alumni associations and clubs.
- Become an associate member of an organization linked to your industry.
- Give something back to your community by getting involved. Volunteer to help out at charitable organizations, local fundraisers, sporting events, church events, art festivals or anything for which you have a passion.
- Give your expertise away for free—give a speech or write an article—and become better known for the right reasons.
- It's not the mistake that matters; it's the recovery. Turn mistakes into networking opportunities.

- Use your judgment when networking on an airplane. Introduce yourself when you first sit down, but respect people's right to privacy if their body language indicates they don't want to talk. Use the meal for networking.

- Learn from the princes of networking when creating your own in-house networking events—have rich content, a thoughtful mix of people and interesting venues.

- Create a networking culture in your work environment; share contact information with everyone, support employees' networking efforts and follow up.

- Create a door opener, not gatekeeper, philosophy in your work environment.

- Keep an open mind and network up, down and at the same level. Don't assess a networking event on the CEO quotient or assume that the guest of honor does not want to meet you.

- Be bold and take risks. Introduce yourself to people you want to meet. Sit with them at the lunch table and talk to them.

- If you come to an event with a group, spread out and meet other people.

SUMMARY: continued

- The best way to ask a question:
  - Sit near the front, at the corner away from the podium.
  - Write down your question and read it if you aren't comfortable winging it.
  - Try to be one of the first hands up.
  - Speak clearly and loudly so everyone can hear the question.
  - You have 28 seconds.
  - Ask a straightforward, one-part question.
  - No personal soapboxes, please.
  - Introduce yourself and your organization.
  - If it's an international conference, state your country as well.

R

CHAPTER EIGHT

repeat, repeat, repeat

Being There

Once upon a time, a keen green chorus frog named Tad Pole attended his monthly Chamber of Commerce Amphibians' Night. Tad was a regular at this networking pond and others.

At the event, an ornate horned frog named Emerald drew him to one side and said, "Tad, don't you know if you kiss too many frogs you will get warts?" So concerned was Tad, he went to see his doctor the next day.

"Doctor, is it true, if I kiss too many frogs I will get warts?" he asked.

"No, Tad, it is not true," replied the doctor.

"What will I get, then?" asked Tad, still concerned. "Nothing. Just tired, and a lot of good contacts," replied the wise old doctor.

REPEAT, REPEAT, REPEAT

What do all great networkers have in common, besides being seekers and purveyors of knowledge? "Being there" is at the top of the list.

Great networkers make a habit of going to events. They accept invitations, buy tickets and show up. Their first instinct is to say yes. By being there, great networkers develop good reputations and are well respected.

WENDY AND SONJA

Wendy McDonald and Sonja Bata come to mind immediately when I think about being there.

Both are great—no, remarkable—networkers. They are tireless supporters of their own businesses and local communities, and they travel constantly around the world. They are gracious and charming. I am sure they get tired of their rigorous schedules, but to them, networking is not a chore. It's what they do—and what is absolutely amazing is that they are doing it in their seventies and eighties. They are an inspiration to all of us.

WENDY

Wendy McDonald is a networking royal. She has built her business success in great part due to her exceptional networking skills. She has run her hundred-million-dollar-plus multi-national company, U.S. Bearings, for the past fifty years. She has won countless awards, including the prestigious "*Veuve Clicquot* Award of Distinction," given each year to the top businesswoman in a different country. She has survived three husbands, is a mother of ten and had twenty-eight grandchildren at last count.

In her early thirties, Wendy was left a widow with three young children when her first husband died in a plane crash. She was also left with her husband's small, struggling machine shop and bearing-supply company. Wendy had no business experience, but she also had no choice. She needed to work to survive.

Women in management in the 1950s were highly unusual, particularly in the male-dominated ball-bearing business. Wendy persevered, surviving a management revolt and other hardships. The key to her success has always been her understanding of the importance of building relationships through networking. That's what Wendy has done throughout her fifty-year career: built and maintained strong relationships with her employees, suppliers, customers, associates and friends. She's a complete natural at it, and I speak from experience.

TIME ZONES BE DAMNED

As the chief hired hand of The Board of Trade, each year I work with an elected chairperson who is a leading member of the business community. When Wendy was chair, I traveled with her on a number of trade missions to Asia and Europe. She has always been one of my favorite tag-team partners.

On one of those trade missions to Asia—ten countries in the same number of days—there she was, wearing a new outfit every day, always ready to go, attending every factory tour, every lunch, every reception and dinner in those wilting climates. She wore me out. As I said good-bye to her in Manila, I went home to recover as she took off on a tour to see her Asian customers. From Wendy, I've learned you have to meet a lot of frogs—time zones be damned.

SONJA

Tom Bata and his wife Sonja have built the Bata Shoe Company into one of the world's most global companies. Founded in 1894 in Czechoslovakia with the aim "to shoe the world," that's exactly what it did. The company manufactures, distributes and retails a wide range of shoes on five continents, from the most rudimentary styles to high fashion.

Tom and Sonja are a great tag-team. Sonja is a businesswoman, philanthropist and founder of the unique Bata Shoe Museum. Like her husband, she travels the world visiting Bata shoe factories and stores in seventy-four countries.

I feel part of Sonja's small-world network because I bump into her all the time—in airline lounges, New York hotel lobbies or even dockside, greeting a warship returning from the Persian Gulf, resplendent in her uniform as an honorary Navy captain. She has the gift of grace and is always genuinely interested in meeting people, be they young Navy recruits or heads of state. She treats everyone as equals. Like Wendy, she is indefatigable.

DAVE AND YVONNE

Dave Roels and Yvonne DeValone are two outstanding networkers. While they may not run big international organizations like Wendy and Sonja, they are well known and respected in their own spheres. They have built their businesses and developed excellent reputations by "being there." They exemplify the power of positive networking.

DAVE

One day, a photographer named Dave Roels came to see me, hoping I'd help him establish his credentials as a corporate photographer. I invited him to take some pictures at an upcoming event. When I've made that offer to other photographers, they've made themselves available only for large events. Dave was different. If I asked Dave to shoot an event, large or small, he was always available.

At one event, I asked him if he would do a portrait of our guest speaker, the prime minister of Thailand. Dave saw an opportunity, took the portrait on the spot and, from then on, was ready with a mini portrait studio for every major speaker. Over the years, he has assembled an impressive portfolio of portraits of business leaders and world figures, including Chris Patten, the last governor of Hong Kong, Bob Crandall, chairman of American Airlines, and anthropologist Jane Goodall, to mention a few.

While skill and knowledge are essential, being there is a necessary requirement for success, as Dave's case proves.

YVONNE

Yvonne DeValone is a dynamo who owns a very successful storage business. A leading member of my organization, she participates in many committees and activities. I see her at events at least once a week, often more. A while back, when I hadn't seen Yvonne for a couple of months, I asked where she had been. She said she was "burned out" and had decided to drop networking for a month or so.

Then she told me that when she stopped networking, her new business dropped by fifty percent. That's why she was back, and she was happy to report that business was rising accordingly. For Yvonne, advertising and marketing aren't as effective as her skilled approach to positive networking and just being there.

NUGGET You've got to put in the effort to make it effortless.

Wendy, Sonja, Dave and Yvonne make positive networking part of their everyday routine. They've made the network dance part of what they do. They get it.

DOUBTING THOMAS

Thomas, a student in one of my executive MBA seminars, defined networking as "standing around making small talk and thinking how much more productive I could be if I were back at my office." This is not an unusual view. Here's what I told him.

"Set a goal of attending just one networking event a week. That's forty-seven events a year—with five weeks off for good behavior. And make seven good contacts per event. Then do the arithmetic. At the end of the year you'll have 329 new contacts—1,645 at the end of five years. Could this happen sitting at your desk? I don't think so."

Actually, it isn't 1,645 contacts at the end of five years, it is 1,645 new networks—the incredible shrinking world.

START YOUNG

Established business people aren't the only ones who sometimes question the importance of networking. To people just starting out in business, networking is the furthest thing from their minds. Thirty-year-olds may think, "Hey, networking is for old geezers." This attitude is particularly prevalent in nontraditional business environments, where *foosball*, not golf, is the office sport of choice. Employees there can't picture themselves hobnobbing with a bunch of "suits."

But it's the perfect time to start. Adding three hundred and twenty-nine new contacts to your circle each year builds a powerful network. Under-thirties should be thinking, "Where is that next event? I'm there."

BETTER LATE THAN NEVER

On the other end of the spectrum, where is it written that you have to give up networking when you retire? The answer is: it isn't, and you don't. Remember Russell Benson, the "somewhat retired livestock buyer?"

WORDS OF WISDOM

Samuel Johnson, the famous eighteenth-century English writer, once said, "If a man does not make new acquaintances as he advances through life, he will soon find himself left alone. A man, sir, should keep his friendship in a constant repair."

I think this quote is as applicable today as it was in the 1700s. Building and maintaining a circle of contacts become even more important as you get older. Engage in at least one activity a week where you meet new people, and your circle of contacts will continue to expand and be maintained.

Ask yourself what your current network of contacts looks like and what you want it to look like in ten years. How about in twenty years?

Want something to strive for? Wendy McDonald had four hundred friends at her eightieth birthday party—friends from just one city who were able to make it.

WHOLE LOT OF NETWORKIN' GOING ON

All this "repeat, repeat, repeat" doesn't come without pitfalls. Just showing up isn't enough. We've got to contribute something besides our mere presence. Networking is about the exchange of knowledge and information. Good networkers are seekers and purveyors of knowledge. Your thoughts needn't always be profound, but your opinions need to be based on fact; for that, you will be respected. So you've got to know something.

LIFE-LONG LEARNING

Knowing something means more than having good general knowledge. It all starts with natural curiosity. Knowledge is at your fingertips. Use the resources of the Internet, including online courses.

There are other ways to expand your horizons. Enroll in mid-career courses, such as an executive MBA program or community college courses, to improve your knowledge and skill. The bonus is you are exposed to new people and their networks. Relying on what you learned in college isn't enough. Knowing something requires a commitment to life-long learning.

NUGGET

Learning is not compulsory... neither is survival.
—Dr. W. Edwards Deming
Engineer and quality guru

ASK AND YOU SHALL FIND

Ask a question and you usually find out something interesting. That is one of Gayle's secrets to being a good conversationalist. She is genuinely interested in learning something new, and her theory is that everyone knows something she doesn't know. "I only need to ask a few questions to find out a person's passion, or their area of expertise. Then I ask their opinion on something related. People love to talk about what they care about."

She can keep the conversation going because of her wide range of knowledge. When I see her stack of reading materials, ranging from *The Economist* and *Foreign Affairs* to *Vanity Fair* and *People*, I understand why she knows something about just about everything.

DIALOGUE AND DIPLOMACY

At an international conference in Switzerland, Gayle and I hosted a small dinner party for Mary Robinson, president of Ireland. I sat at one end of the table with the president, and Gayle sat at the other end with the Irish ambassador to the United Nations.

At her end, Gayle was deep in conversation. She had attended several conference sessions on the UN and she knew the issues. After a while, I noticed that the ambassador was leaning over, listening to her intently—and *he was taking notes.*

Later that evening I asked Gayle why the ambassador was writing notes during their conversation. She matter-of-factly replied, "He was interested in my ideas on marketing the United Nations to the public."

Although she says it was just a coincidence, over the next couple of years, the UN implemented a number of things she had suggested, including a public awareness campaign that used actors like Jeremy Irons as UN ambassadors-at-large. I may be biased, but I prefer to give Gayle *all* the credit.

The moral? As a knowledgeable conversationalist, you should feel comfortable enough to speak up.

THE CONVERSATION CHAIN

Just as you have permission to network, and others have permission to network with you, everyone has permission to speak up. It is one way to evolve from passenger to participant.

While you should not categorize anyone too quickly—just like the frog chain—you can rank *yourself* in the conversation chain.

THE ACTIVE PARTICIPANT

A contributor. You take the lead, ask thoughtful questions, engage issues and involve others in the conversation.

THE ACTIVE PASSENGER

You are attentive, ask easy questions, have cards and offer some comments.

THE PASSIVE PASSENGER

You nod occasionally, may smile, don't have cards and rarely speak.

JUST BAGGAGE

You nod off, don't speak, don't want cards and would rather be watching *Wheel of Fortune.*

If you aren't an active participant or active passenger, it's time to raise the bar for yourself. It's a long life, and more fun if you get involved and become a real player.

THE SEVENTH SECRET OF NETWORKING

The seventh secret of networking isn't two secrets; it's one: « **Be there and know something.** » You can't network effectively from behind your desk; you've got to meet people. And there's no point *being there* unless you have something to contribute beyond your presence. Read, listen, seek out knowledge and share it.

SUMMARY

repeat, repeat, repeat

- Repeat, repeat, repeat—the more networking you do, the better you get at it. The better you are at it, the more positive the results.
- Great networkers work on building relationships and are known for being there. They make it part of their everyday life, and develop a reputation for reliability.
- Start networking now, no matter what your age or circumstances—under thirty, over forty, stay-at-home, retrenched, retired.
- Go to just one event a week, meet seven new people, and in a year you will have a pool of over three hundred contacts.
- Being there is important not only for making new contacts, but for maintaining existing ones.
- Don't be a one-pond wonder. Have a depth of contacts in your specialized pond, but expand your horizons by building contacts in many ponds.
- Just being there is not enough. You need to know something because positive networking is about the exchange of knowledge and information.

SUMMARY: continued

- You have permission to speak up, so be an active participant or active passenger.
- Some of the most extraordinary networkers are still going strong in their seventies and eighties.

CHAPTER NINE

keep it going

"Frog-ot"

Once upon a time in the town of Greensboro lived an Eastern banjo frog named Joey. He was getting ready for his first Rotary meeting after a summer at the family pond in the Smoky Mountains. He felt the chill of winter coming on so he put on his nice "weed" jacket.

Joey put his hand in his pocket and found a big wad of business cards that he had collected at a networking event last winter, at the Caddis Inn. Overcome with reptilian regret, he realized that he had just "frog-ot" to call some of these frogs. He'd even promised to send an article to one of them.

He wondered if he'd bump into any of them at the event tonight. Would they remember that he wasn't a frog of his word?

KEEP IT GOING

Alchemy is the mythical science of transforming lead into gold, but the science of networking is real, and it creates a truly small world for those who participate. Skillful application of the art of positive networking can convert a worthless stack of business cards into a *golden* network of fine frogs, princes and princesses. Without follow-up, the fruits of networking labors are no more than stacks of business cards littering our desk drawers and lying fallow in our jacket pockets.

Follow-up is the only way to develop new relationships and create closer bonds in all circles of contacts—acquaintances, extended and close. It starts by putting into practice that most important secret of networking—discovering something you can do for someone else. Follow-up then requires the patience and interest to find out what that "something" could be.

DO IT

When you find out what that something is, it's not enough to think about it—do it. Big or small, if the gesture is sincere, it will be memorable, and possibly very important to the other person. And guess what? You may have just transformed yourself into someone's prince or princess.

BEST INTENTIONS

Who hasn't heard stories of someone who pulled out all the stops to do something for someone else? Who hasn't experienced someone surprising them with a kind, follow-up gesture? How about the photo someone sent from an event you both attended, or the call made on your behalf to help you with a job search?

We are more often reminded of follow-ups that didn't happen, because even with the best of intentions to follow up, human beings get tripped up.

- We mean to send a brief email to someone we met the night before—we hit it off so well. But the next day it didn't seem that important.

- We know we promised to invite someone to an event we are hosting, and now we can't remember; who was that person?

- We diligently put a person's card in our contact list, and then we don't do anything with it.

- We find it harder and harder to come up with a reason to call or email a contact we made months ago. A year later, as we are cleaning up our email list, we hit "delete" when we see their name.

BE RELIABLE

The first way to deal with "best intentions" is to make a commitment to become more reliable. Reliability builds your reputation—your good reputation. Return phone calls or emails by the next day. Follow up promptly on leads. If you promise to do something, do it right away. You'll become known as a person who gets things done.

NUGGET

Be reliable. If you say you will do it, do it. Do it sooner rather than later.

BEYOND THE CALL OF DUTY

Prompt follow-up can be overdone. At least, it appeared that way to me. The week before leaving on a trade mission to Indonesia, I had been trying to connect with my good friend, Dr. John Wiebe, president of the Asia Pacific Foundation. His organization arranges the world-famous GLOBE Foundation environmental conferences, and I needed key information from him to prepare my remarks as a moderator for one of the conference's panel discussions. Despite much telephone tag, and the fact that we worked only two floors apart, my attempts to connect with him were unsuccessful.

I boarded the airplane, frustrated, and arrived in Bali twenty-nine hours later. I crashed—figuratively speaking—on the soft white sand beach at the Nua Dusa Hotel overlooking the Indian Ocean. I awoke with a start from my equatorial slumber; someone was kicking my foot. "Rezac, you were calling me. What can I do for you?"

There, silhouetted eerily against the hot tropical sun, stood John Wiebe. In my groggy state, I wondered if he had traveled to the other side of the world just to return my call. That would have been follow-up beyond the call of duty. Actually, he was on his way to visit GLOBE sponsors in Australia, and had stopped in Bali to break up the trip. Small world.

YOU NEED A SYSTEM

To be really good at follow-up, you need a system. How else are you going to manage all those new contacts, follow up on commitments and keep your network active?

NUGGET

It's not what you know that gets you into trouble. It's what you know that ain't so.

—Bill Rich, Master fly fisherman

It's not the stuff you know; it's the stuff you don't know, or the stuff you have forgotten, that gets you into trouble. Get into the habit of carrying a small notebook with you, or using your Palm Pilot, BlackBerry or other handheld device to jot down things you've promised others. Most of us don't possess a photographic memory. Write it down so you won't forget. Prepare to jog your memory by writing the date and name of the event on the back of the cards you have collected. Do this as soon as possible after the event. The back of the card is also a handy place to write down other reminders.

KILLER APPLICATION

Riffling through stacks of business cards to find the one you want is a time waster if ever there was one. Besides, Murphy's Law dictates that the business card you want is always at the bottom of the last stack you look through.

There is a great solution to organizing your business cards. It's called the card scanner. It's the killer application of networking. You simply put a business card in your card scanner; it enters data into the correct fields and synchronizes with your contact-organizing list. Unlike a Rolodex, which has a finite amount of space, a card scanner can keep all the cards you want. Back up this information; it's your networking lifeline. For networking purposes, the card scanner is the greatest invention since...well, since business cards.

TECHNO-PEASANT

If you are highly visual and need to see and touch the cards, or if you are a techno-peasant and proud of it, there's a solution for you as well. Use binders with clear sheets specifically designed to hold business cards. Organize them in a way that makes sense to you—and the sooner after the event, the better.

LEARN SOMETHING

You've got a person's card, you've organized it, now what do you do with it? Learn more about the person and his or her company. This may sound time-consuming, especially if you have made the commitment to attend one networking event a week. You know the potential number of cards you collect per year will be in the hundreds. How do you manage this?

Relax. First, you won't be getting all these cards at once. And remember, you aren't starting from scratch. When you first exchanged cards with these people, you traded tribal stories, right? The stories were so interesting that both of you wanted to find out more about each other, but you were circulating in the pond, so you had to move on.

Web sites are great places to get valuable information for follow-up. You'll gain a better understanding of a person's business and may even find out more about the person you've just met. Do it immediately; otherwise these preliminary connections will become "best intentions."

> **NUGGET** People do business with those they know and trust.

SMALL-WORLD PHENOMENON

Another easy way to find out more about a person is to tell friends or associates about the people you've met. Why? Because there's a high probability someone you speak with knows this person. So ask the question, "Do you know……?" Follow-up is a lot easier when you have a common thread joining you to someone else.

KNOW SOMETHING

Why do a lot of groundwork on someone you've just met? Peter Legge, a great networker and awarding-winning public speaker, offers some sage advice in his recent book, *Who Dares Wins*, in quoting his mentor and friend, Joe Segal, who said: "The statement, 'It's not what you know, but who you know' is incorrect. If you don't know anything, you won't know anyone."

It is a bit of a brainteaser, but his point is simple. You need to do your homework and know something, so people will want to know you. Be a good listener, read, seek out knowledge and share it. It's the difference between having nothing to say and being able to say:

- "I read an article in our industry magazine that you might find interesting."
- "After we chatted, I downloaded your software, and…"
- "After our brief conversation, I went on your web site and found out more about…."

NETWORKING IS A CONTACT SPORT

You are now on the road to establishing a connection. Developing that connection needs ongoing follow-up, which demands face-to-face contact on a regular basis. Networking is a contact sport.

How do you do that? If you've met someone at an event on a certain topic, chances are you will see him or her at a similar event. You go to a talk on technology, and the next time the technology association hosts a luncheon,

NUGGET

Networking in its various forms is an art, a science, a contact sport, a skill and a dance.

—Bob Wiens

Businessman and community leader

you'll see some of the same people there. If they have a membership in that organization, it's even more likely you'll see them again.

Follow-up is not a "stalking exercise," it's a matter of being there. Good networkers make it a habit to go to business events as well as fundraisers, service clubs, volunteer organizations and community events. Those are the kinds of events where one can reacquaint themselves with people they've met before. Follow-up is a slow and steady process; patience is required. It's not something you can force.

INSTANT CONNECTION

While some relationships are built slowly over a series of months or years, sometimes two people hit it off immediately. In that case, why wait for fate or the next scheduled event to bring you together again? Invite that person out for coffee, lunch or as your guest to an event. If you've initiated the invitation, be the host—you pay. It's often the way a return engagement happens, with the other person saying, "It's my turn next."

DEAD HORSE

Remember that not all follow-up is successful, nor should it be. You've sent a follow-up email to someone; he doesn't reply. You've chatted with someone off and on, but have never found common ground. You are interested in knowing someone better, but it appears the feeling is not mutual. It may take time to find this out, but during the process, bear in mind that good manners enhance your reputation.

How other people treat you may be beyond your control, but in this situation, it's best to take heed of some very fine advice from a friend, philosopher and cattleman, Dr. Owen Anderson: "If your horse is dead, dismount."

FOLLOW UP WITH CARE

If your horse isn't dead, and you've established a connection with someone, it's important to touch base regularly. This is done by all manner of communication—it is done best when it is done well. That means respecting the space and time of busy people and using the social graces.

Sending everyone you met the night before a handwritten note, gift or brochures, or turning a new email contact into your pen pal, is not appropriate.

Before sending communication to a budding acquaintance, ask yourself, "Is what I am about to send going to add any value to this busy person's life?"

EMAIL CONNECTS THE WORLD

Most of us love the ease and immediacy of email. Some of the best networkers use email all the time, and it's particularly effective for global contacts. It keeps even long-distance contacts warm. It requires only a line or two now and again to keep that connection going.

While email offers a great way to follow up, if it is abused, it can become annoying, and ultimately ignored. There is a mind-boggling amount of information on email etiquette, but a friend, Nigel Protter, has some tips worth sharing. Nigel is a 21st Century Renaissance man and a student of networking. He is beyond computer literacy. Actually, he is completely intolerant of computer illiteracy. Here are his rules for follow-up by email:

- Greet the recipient properly with a polite or warm salutation: "Dear Mr. Protter" (not "Mr. Protter") or "Hi Nigel" (not "Nigel").

- Be succinct and targeted; stay to a single subject with each email. Write a clear subject line. Practice the lost art of précis; chop, chop, chop, but don't be terse. Restrict your follow-up message to two short paragraphs.

- Many people will not open attachments from strangers. Never send photos or other large attachments unless you know the recipient will accept them.

- Photos should be reduced to a maximum of 640x480 pixels each, and then compressed to nothing over 150 KB in total. If someone wants an enlargement or higher-quality version of a photo, they'll ask.

- "Send" is forever. Correct your spelling and grammar. Use the spell checker in your email program. Avoid forwarding or "cc'ing" jokes, poems, virus hoaxes, petitions, chain letters or other time-wasting stuff.

- If you need to forward emails to others, be aware that the previous recipients' email addresses will be passed on in the text of the email. Before forwarding, consider deleting them from the body of the email.

- Do not send anything you wouldn't want to see on the front page of *The New York Times* with your name associated with it.

LOW-TECH FOLLOW UP

Sometimes you need to break the cycle of send and reply. Pick up the phone and have a real live conversation, or invite that person for coffee or lunch. Good networkers make calls just to say hello, or arrange to get together on a regular basis. Communicate the old-fashioned way—it still works best.

WHEN THE PEN IS MIGHTIER THAN THE "SEND"

I am known as an old-fashioned kind of guy because I have made it a habit throughout my career to send handwritten notes. A handwritten note is a nice touch meant as a special thank you, congratulations or personal comment. Use this option selectively, but without hesitation. People usually appreciate the extra effort; and it is a memorable gesture.

If you have children, encourage them to show their appreciation by sending a thank-you note when someone does something nice for them. It is a social grace that will help them build networks throughout their lives.

Whatever your method of follow-up, it requires consistency and attention to detail. Learn how your contacts like to communicate. Some people like phone calls; others can't live without email. Try to use their preferred method for your follow-up.

INSTANT FOLLOW UP

I am also known for my slavish devotion to my BlackBerry. Any PDA, such as Pocket PC or Palm, offers a great tool for instant follow-up when an opportunity presents itself. And opportunities present themselves when you least expect it.

I was using "the power of questions" when I directed an international trade question to the U.S. trade ambassador, Robert Zoellick, at a meeting at the headquarters of the U.S.

Chamber of Commerce in Washington, D.C. Initially, his response was calm and direct, but as he continued, his tone became agitated. Clearly, he had a message that went beyond my question. He was delivering his perspective on sensitive issues of free trade, and he was not happy.

I promptly wrote up his comments on my BlackBerry, and had them posted on The Board of Trade website within an hour, complete with a press release. My story was carried in a national newspaper the next morning. This resulted in a flurry of bilateral diplomatic meetings to pursue the issues Ambassador Zoellick had raised twenty-four hours before.

I doubt the story would have made it into print without the power of modern technology. As it was, an important dialogue between two key trading partners was facilitated through an opportunity taken and made possible by the marvels of technology. Later in the conference, the ambassador was extremely gracious and apologized for "taking it out" on me.

PERMISSION TO FOLLOW UP

If you haven't kept in touch with someone, then use a "permission-to-follow-up" opportunity to restart the connection. Just like "permission-to-network" events there are "permission-to-follow-up" occasions. Christmas, Hanukkah, Thanksgiving and Chinese New Year are such times. You don't need a reason; the event is the reason.

In fact, holidays and special events are a good time to follow up with everyone, not just long-lost friends and acquaintances. Most people take time off during the holiday season to socialize. Plan a luncheon or party or send a card.

Reunions are a great way to follow up with people from your past. Everyone has gone their separate ways over the decades, and they have developed networks in various cities, countries, industries and experiences. If kept active, these networks can be powerful indeed.

Other permission-to-follow-up opportunities can be found in the newspaper. Job promotions, career changes or a flattering newspaper article on someone you know offers you a chance to send a note of congratulations or pick up the phone. Your network is always on. It doesn't take very much follow-up to recharge a connection.

TRUST, A SHARED ASSET

Follow-up is the continuum of all networking exchanges. The real rewards come when you build strong and deep bonds with the people in your network.

Bonds become deeper the longer you know and trust a person. David Dodge, governor of the Bank of Canada, knows something about the value of trust. He says, "Trust is a shared asset; it's confidence that people will do what they say they will do." Bonds are strengthened when two people are like-minded—givers, not takers. They are participants and contributors, the kind of people who know how to get things done.

Often the deepest bonds are developed when you work on high-purpose projects. The enthusiasm of a group of citizens working on a campaign to build a new wing of a library or hospital creates strong bonds because it is something everyone truly cares about. There is a powerful synergy when people are committed to helping their community.

TEAM SPIRIT

I see this all the time at our own organization. Highly respected members of the business community volunteer to lead The Board of Trade for a year. These are very busy people who add the duty to already hectic schedules. We work them very hard. They invest time and money (this is a non-paid position). They attend early-morning executive meetings, hold press conferences on public policy, chair luncheons, host evening events and travel on trade missions, all while continuing to run their business enterprises.

After their year as chair, they may think they are too exhausted to repeat the process immediately, but they don't stop. The next year, I often note they've taken on the chairmanship of a charitable foundation or university board, or committed time and resources to any number of high-purpose volunteer organizations. And they continue to stay connected with our organization. Doing so, they build and maintain strong and useful networks. Community participation is not a one-shot deal for positive networkers.

LIFE LONG PURSUIT

Follow-up doesn't show instant results in most cases. It is a life long commitment. The dynamics of how networks work means that if you invest the time and energy in positive follow-up, you will create something substantially more powerful than most of us can imagine.

Sometimes we all need a "little help from our friends." And when you ask your network for help the results can be quite spectacular. In return, all you need to do is be willing to help others.

THE TIES THAT BIND

The launch of Rocky Mountaineer Railtours, which offers one of the world's most spectacular train trips, is one of those stories. It's a tale about the power of networks, and it's a story Judy knows well. She was there at the start.

When she left the world of accounting to run off and join the railroad, she had no idea what she was getting herself into as the company's first director of customer service. She started on a Friday the 13th. It was a sign of things to come.

An inexperienced and somewhat motley crew had only six weeks to get the company ready for its inaugural train trip through the Rockies. The firm had the train cars, but not much else—no employees, uniforms or suppliers—and a very tight budget.

Within days of joining, the president, Peter Armstrong, told Judy and the team, "There's been a *slight* change of plans. Our inaugural trip isn't going to happen in six weeks, it's going to happen next week."

They couldn't say no to four hundred high-profile train-savvy tourism marketers. The lean management team was short on experience, but long on friends. Peter had a particularly extensive network of contacts that he conscripted into service, as did his managers. Phones were working overtime as networks upon networks were mobilized.

Seven days later, the train pulled out of the station with the most eclectic group of train lovers a railway has ever seen. Working this first run were retired railroad executives, marketing vice presidents, media consultants, business advisors and lawyers. Accountants, flight attendants, brothers, sisters and wives, all dressed in rented tuxedos, had been commandeered to serve as the onboard service attendants. And they were all loving it, as were the guests.

One vice president's brother, an electrical engineer *and* medical doctor, served drinks to his passengers and handled medical emergencies. "Dr. Doug" would later don overalls, grab his voltmeter and help fix the train when mechanical problems arose, passengers cheering as the train returned to service. Rocky Mountaineer Railtours is now a world-class rail tour company that carries thousands of passengers from all over the globe every year.

Peter had a strong network and he activated it in an emergency. This mind-boggling last-minute launch could never have happened if he hadn't tapped into the power of his network.

> **NUGGET**
> As the song goes... "with a little help from your friends" you can more than just "get by."

A VOYAGE OF DISCOVERY

There is no guarantee that you will sell more widgets or climb to the top of a corporate ladder as a result of becoming a good networker. But one thing I can guarantee you: Your chances are a heck of a lot better.

It is a voyage of discovery that consists of seeing networking through new eyes, because you have understood that it is not all about you—it's about discovering what you can do for others. This establishes your network, and because of it you will be able to do amazing things. This is the most rewarding aspect of the whole voyage.

> **NUGGET**
> We must learn to see the world anew.
> —Albert Einstein

A SCHOOL FOR A DOLLAR

It happened to me, Peter and Mickey. Peter Hammer is a financial advisor, community volunteer and director of the Fraser Academy, a school for one hundred and seventy students with dyslexia and language-based learning disabilities. The school rented space on a site owned by a large multinational brewery, Molson. The brewery was being moved and the land was being turned into a condominium project. The school would have to move.

Peter came to see me, very worried. "Darcy," he said, "I have to talk to Mickey Cohen, can you help me?" Mickey Cohen, president of Molson, was scheduled to be the guest speaker at our luncheon the following week. I told Peter to come along and I'd introduce him to Mickey to see what could be done.

Peter came to the event, and I introduced them after the lunch. Peter told his story and found Mickey more receptive than he had imagined. In a matter of seconds I could see it was an energized connection. Within a matter of weeks, Molson gave the buildings occupied by the school to the city, and the city leased them back to the Fraser Academy for a dollar a year.

IT TAKES A NETWORK

This story illustrates the power of positive networking. Both Peter and Mickey had a strong desire to do something for someone else. Mickey wanted to do something for the community after the disruption of moving the plant with its high-paying jobs. Peter was already a participant and contributor in his community, and he knew to go to his network for help. My job was easy; I was just the connector. And because everyone followed up on what they said they would do, the school was saved.

Here, the magic of positive networking involved just three handshakes that made all the difference in the world to one hundred and seventy students.

« The magic of positive networking is all around us: It's in the people, it's in the dance, it's in the secrets. »

SUMMARY

keep it going

- To be a good networker, you need to be good at follow-up.
- Follow-up is all about discovering what you can do for someone else, and doing it. That's how you develop and form relationships.
- You need to learn something about people before you can discover what you can do for them. Ask questions, research their company's web site and talk with others. It's a small world, and people are connected.
- Build your good "follow-up" reputation. Be reliable, trustworthy and prompt. Be a person who gets things done.
- Get organized. Carry a small notebook, Palm Pilot or other handheld device and use it to keep track of commitments.
- Organize your contacts by using a card scanner. Get rid of those little bundles of cards all over your desk.
- Networking is a contact sport. You need face-to-face contact on a regular basis to build connections.

SUMMARY: continued

- Follow up with care. Use email etiquette, communicate information of value and use gifts and notes appropriately. Be memorable for the right reasons.

- Use "permission-to-follow-up" holidays and events to establish links with old acquaintances in addition to your extended and close contacts.

- Get involved—participate, invite someone to an event, share experiences. Follow-up allows you to keep the bonds in your networks strong.

- Remember, not all follow-up is successful. That's okay. So if your horse is dead—dismount.

- Expand your contacts beyond your small circle to include different industries, organizations, cities and countries. Science shows that a few highly connected people can link a large number of not-so-well-connected people. That's the power of networks and small worlds.

CHAPTER TEN

happily ever after

The End of the Beginning

Once upon a time, there was an arboreal forest frog named Socrates. Like his namesake 2,500 years earlier, he was a teacher and mentor to many, including his younger sister Lily.

Socrates taught Lily the secrets of positive networking and coached her through the seven steps of the network dance. The buzz and croaking that came from a full chorus of frogs, and even the odd knot of toads, made him feel alive. The din of the room was always music to his ears—such as they were. And Lily was a quick study.

Socrates helped Lily overcome some challenging hurdles. Just thinking about networking used to get Lily all tongue-tied. For a frog this can be a very serious thing. Socrates had her sign up for Croak Masters International to deal with her paralyzing fear of public ribbiting. Soon she came to enjoy meeting a group of strangers and even standing up in a crowd and speaking out.

Once, when she encountered a networking setback and was rebuffed, Socrates asked her, "Whose problem is it when someone decides that

YOU WILL NEVER EVER BE ABLE TO DO SOMETHING FOR THEM?"

HER ANSWER TO THIS AND THE MYRIAD OF OTHER QUESTIONS SOCRATES POSED IN HIS TUTORING—SUCH WAS HIS METHOD—SOON GAVE LILY THE CONFIDENCE TO STRIKE OUT ON HER OWN. SHE WAS KEEN TO APPLY HER NEWFOUND KNOWLEDGE AND SEE WHAT SHE COULD DO FOR OTHERS.

SHE ASKED SOCRATES, "WHAT ADVICE CAN YOU GIVE ME ON MY VOYAGE OF DISCOVERY?"

SOCRATES REPLIED, "PREPARE YOURSELF FOR EVERY DAY—READ, ASK QUESTIONS, LISTEN. THE VOYAGE OF DISCOVERY NEVER ENDS. ALWAYS BE AWARE OF THE NETWORK AND ITS REACH; IT IS ALWAYS ON. UNDERSTAND THAT POSITIVE NETWORKING FLOWS FROM THE SECRETS AND STEPS OF THE NETWORK DANCE. THEREFORE, PRACTICE, PRACTICE, PRACTICE. FINALLY, PARTICIPATE AND BE A CONTRIBUTOR. IN TIME, YOU—AND THOSE YOU TOUCH—WILL EXPERIENCE THE MAGIC OF THE RANDOM AND UNEXPECTED GOOD THINGS THAT WILL COME FROM POSITIVE NETWORKING DONE WELL."

HAPPILY EVER AFTER

After the better part of two decades in the networking arena, and after observing some of the world's best at work, I continue to be amazed by the prevailing state of the art. First, I am amazed at how few great networkers there really are, how scarce the good ones are, and generally how reluctant people are to network. Too many—by their own admission—just don't like it or don't believe in it.

This book is a lesson in *network shepa*, or the awareness of the power of positive networking. And the power is real. Not only have successful leaders and achievers known this from the beginning of time, but recent science has also proved the remarkable strength of *the six degrees of separation phenomenon*—the fact that we are connected to everyone else by only a few handshakes.

The Frog and Prince shares the secrets and steps essential to making you a better networker. Amongst them is a positive networking secret that has made my organization famous, *the password to the network: permission.* Give yourself, and everyone with whom you come in contact, permission to network. The multiplier effect is astonishing.

Personal networking is not an exact science, but one basic fact is immutable. If you are to be successful at it, you have to network a lot. That's the secret: *You have to kiss a lot of frogs to find a prince.*

Possibly the most important secret of positive networking is, it's not all about you. It's about the people with whom you come in contact. Positive networks are created and sustained *when we discover something we can do for someone else.* It has to do with our close and extended circle of contacts—

even acquaintances are important—and our ties with them. And the power of it all comes from the networking magic of *small-worlds,* the random and unexpected good things that happen to those who have learned both the secrets and the network dance well, and those whom they touch.

While discovering what you can do for someone and granting permission to network are about attitude, some secrets of positive networking are as simple as shifting behavior. Always, always *introduce yourself, carry business cards and give them out as a matter of routine.* Too many people do not even carry business cards. Make sure you are not amongst them. It's an important and fundamental part of the network dance.

The same holds true for the s*ecret of asking questions,* in both small meetings and large public gatherings. This secret may require you to step outside your comfort zone, but like everything else with training and practice, doing so will become easier. Questions are such a powerful way to introduce yourself and your organization to a large group of people that it's worth the stretch. Asking good questions is also a great conversation starter in smaller settings. Socrates was famous for it.

Another secret of positive networking is also a secret of life—*treat everyone as equals.* Everyone deserves to be treated with dignity, kindness and respect. Avoid rushing to rank your contacts in the frog chain. Besides, one person's frog may be another person's prince or princess. Treating everybody like royalty is a good idea.

The secret that may well be the most difficult for many is, *be there and know something.* To network effectively, you have to jump in and get your feet wet—you have to be there. And there's no point being there unless you have something to contribute beyond your presence. Do your homework and know something. Be a good listener, read, seek out knowledge and share it. If you have to be a passenger, be an engaging one. Being an *active participant* who makes a contribution is even better.

Participants ought not be discouraged when they encounter the occasional inevitable setback. Remember *Network Rule No. 7: Deal with it, get over it and move on.*

If you take only one thing from this book, let it be this: Positive networking works. It can be an incredibly powerful element of our business and personal success. As importantly, it will also benefit others. And the great news is: if we learn the secrets and seven steps of positive networking and do it well, the power is ours. Any one of us can become a *prince or princess of networking.*

the end

SUMMARY

happily ever after

THE SEVEN SECRETS OF POSITIVE NETWORKING

1. You have to kiss a lot of frogs to find a prince.
Kissing frogs is what networking is all about. Make it a matter of habit.

2. Networking is not all about you: It's discovering what you can do for someone else.
Networks are created and sustained when we discover something we can do for someone else. For some, this is a new way of viewing the world, but once realized, networking becomes easier. The pressure is off. You are in the world of positive networking.

3. Introduce yourself by name, always carry business cards and give them out. Make it a habit.
Too many people don't follow this simple advice. Give yourself the advantage. Be someone who does.

4. Treat everyone as equals.
This makes life a whole lot easier than trying to figure out who's who. One person's frog may be another's prince or princess.

5. Give everyone the password to the network: permission.
Give yourself—and everyone you come in contact with—permission to network. The multiplier effect of this simple secret is astonishing.

6. Learn the power of asking questions and use it.
Questions are a powerful way to introduce yourself to a large or small group. Get the training to speak in public and step outside of your comfort zone; it's worth the stretch.

7. Be there and know something.
You can't network effectively from behind your desk; you've got to meet people. And there's no point being there unless you have something to contribute beyond your presence. Read, listen, seek out knowledge and share it.

AFTERWORD

by Dr. Daniel F. Muzyka
Dean and Professor

In a world where ideas, knowledge and resources are constantly turning over and expanding, the ability to identify new opportunities is critical. With *The Frog and Prince: Secrets of Positive Networking*, Darcy has seized an opportunity and run with it. He marries the art and revolutionary new findings in the science of networks in an eminently refreshing and practical way.

As an academic, I too am excited by the research into the power of networks, how they form and how they act—research by Duncan Watts, Steve Strogatz and others. The science of "small-worlds" is heady stuff. Darcy uses this science as a compelling backdrop to underscore his view of the world of personal networks and how they work.

I was heartened to see in print (some for the first time, I might add) many "tricks of the trade" that I have garnered through my years of networking. I have also learned a thing or two, successfully putting to good use half a dozen new suggestions made in this book. It is a practical field-guide to the networking craft.

Darcy has clearly earned his networking stripes. We share a common sense of networking awareness, be it recognition of the importance of cross-cultural differences, or the highly enjoyable activity of the care and feeding of our networks.

The Frog and Prince deserves strong praise as a practitioner's guide to networking, and there are three themes worth repeating. Firstly, through his *opus*, Darcy reminds us that positive networking is not something we do "because we have to." It ought to be a seamless and natural part of a fulfilled life. *The Frog and Prince* reminds us, through stories and illustrations, that in all of our social interactions, we are always networking. Our choice is to do it well or do it poorly. The many lessons in this book can make that difference.

A second theme is that networking is not an end in itself, but a facilitating process for value creation. This fundamental point is made when Darcy notes that networking is "about discovering what we can do for someone else." The key to sustainable networking is value exchange. Those who only "take," or network for the sake of networking (what one of my colleagues refers to as "content-free networking"), should rethink their ideas.

A third theme is that networks are like any other personal or business asset. If we spend little time interacting in social, business and community activities, our network won't disappear, but it will depreciate like any aging asset. Network interaction—especially where we add value through our ideas and support—helps maintain the asset.

Well, how did *The Frog and Prince* fare? Having read the book cover to cover—twice—I give it an "A." Darcy, with the help of Judy and Gayle, has created a book that explains networking in such a way that it makes you want to turn *off* your computer, drop a regular meeting or two, grab some business cards and seek out the first networking opportunity you can find. I recommend it as required reading for anyone who wants to understand the practical aspects of effective networking—students and business practitioners alike.

And it is clear from the enthusiasm evident in both the book and the *Secrets of Positive Networking Seminars* that there is more to come. In the meantime, I hope you take the opportunity to enhance your own ability to create, deliver and share in value by implementing even a few of their worthwhile suggestions. Happy networking!

Daniel F. Muzyka is Dean of the Faculty of Commerce at the University of British Columbia. He was Professor and Associate Dean responsible for the MBA program at INSEAD (France), and has been a Visiting Professor at Harvard, where he received his doctorate. He received an MBA from the Wharton School, and a BA in Astrophysics from Williams College. He represents UBC at the World Economic Forum.

ACKNOWLEDGMENTS

When Gayle, Judy and I met with Peter Legge, author of *Who Dares Wins*, we outlined our ideas for this book. He was unequivocal. "Just do it; you'll never regret it." Peter not only became a welcome champion of the project, but also a role model.

My interest in the art and science of networking spans two decades, and the task of remembering all who shaped my thinking along the way is an impossible one. To those that I've omitted, I apologize.

"Superdean" Dr. Dan Muzyka, a frequent tag-team partner, has been an enthusiastic mentor from the beginning. Not only is he a great networker; he is a superb coach. Dr. Owen Anderson, student of the great Herman Kahn and a philosopher in his own right, has been a colleague for more than twenty-five years. He has provided wisdom and insight that have shaped many of my ideas. His Socratic approach to dialogue—using the power of thoughtful questions—has been highly instructive. Master mediator, lawyer, diplomat, professor and bon vivant Frank Borowicz and his totally engaging wife, family court judge Marilynn, are an awesome tag-team. Gayle, Judy and I have been appreciative recipients of their generosity of spirit. And it was Frank who first introduced me to a supercharged, Cambridge-educated lawyer named Barry Appleton. Barry is now The Board's Honorary Representative in Washington, D.C. He has a vast network of top-level contacts worldwide, and regularly pulls out the stops to help others, including The Board of Trade and me. He was of invaluable assistance on this project.

Two great friends, honorary Navy captain Cedric Steele, and Japan-based Wilf Wakely, have been willing and ebullient confederates throughout. I often get to travel in the slipstream of these world-class raconteurs. Amazing things happen around these guys.

Two people who have been with this project from startup are Bob Wiens and Rob Hamilton. Bob is a successful businessman emeritus and dedicated community leader—he's a *participant and contributor* par excellence. Rob Hamilton is an entrepreneur and chartered accountant who runs a robust wholesale coffee roasting and distributing business. It may have been the caffeine that kept him going, critiquing many drafts of our book, in his dedicated support of our efforts.

We were fortunate to have had a valuable network of gentle (and not so gentle) readers: Jennifer Chapman, Tom Donohue, Peter and Carol Fraser, Ted Garland, Dr. Carl Grant, Jim Matkin, Connie Parsons, Sue Spooner, Jim Robinson and Colleen Rezac. Their advice was vital to achieving the final product. The amount of volunteer effort committed to this project is proof that random and unexpected good things come from your network.

Peter C. Newman, a brilliant historian, planted the seed for this book with his slightly cheeky quote in *Titans.* "Darcy Rezac, who heads The Vancouver Board of Trade, claims he invented networking, it's not true—he only perfected it." Peter and Lyall Knott, his networking buddy, have been my poster boys for empowered networkers. Wait for an event? Not them. They created their own popular series of small networking dinners to introduce prominent out-of-town visitors to the business community.

Norman Stowe and Oona McKinstry of the PACE Group are public affairs masters. They taught me that rather than trying to "think outside the box," just do away with it. Networking royals Michelle Brazeau, Benjamin Colling, Nora Newlands and Robert Noon encouraged me from the beginning. Andrew Reid of Vision Critical created a totally *ribbiting* web home at www.frogandprince.com.

The Vancouver Board of Trade is an amazing place, and few organizations could provide a better crucible in which to observe, experiment, study and practice the art and science of networking. The range of policy issues and international scope of our activities has provided a rich and relevant backdrop for one of the most active speakers' platforms on the continent. The Board's website, *www.boardoftrade.com*, can only scratch the surface of what goes on—and has gone on—for over one hundred and fifteen years. It is a veritable beehive of activity, with close to thirty thousand seats filled at various functions and events each year. Well over two hundred thousand business cards are exchanged every year at The Board.

The enthusiasm, loyalty and volunteer contributions of our members have always impressed me. Amongst those members are many star networkers, too many to mention. But they should know their contribution to the discipline of networking has been invaluable to me. This has been particularly true of the Contact Club, whose members include Bernie Isman, who joined The Board of Trade in 1946. The club meets monthly, and Bernie rarely misses a meeting.

Our directors and chairs, past and present, exemplify the phrase participant and contributor. These are people who give up to one third of their working day to take on weighty volunteer commitments, and they do so unselfishly. Most continue to stay involved with The Board well after their term. These are folks dedicated to their community and to making a difference.

Gayle and Judy have worked tirelessly, almost non-stop, for the better part of a year on this book, snatching time with me here and there, editing my stuff, preparing their drafts, merging ideas and doing all the things that book writers have to do. It truly has been a collaborative effort and it would have been impossible without them. I am lucky to have had them.

Finally this book is dedicated to a very special group of people—the volunteers and staff of The Vancouver Board of Trade with whom I have worked since 1986. In all my time in the public and private sectors, I have never worked with such an incredible group of people. No one who comes into contact with The Board fails to be impressed with the quality, variety, timeliness and relevance of what goes on and the vitality of the people who work and volunteer there. I continue to be amazed at how they pull rabbits out of the hat, day after day, year after year, to make the networking experience for members and their guests second to none. Thank you for what you do and for allowing me to be part of it.

Darcy Rezac
January, 2003

APPENDIX I

TIPS FOR GOOD BUSINESS CARD DESIGN

- Use point sizes that are readable in low light. Here are some examples, using the Times New Roman font:

For your name: 11 point	(Name)
For your title: 10 point	(President)
For contact information: 9 point	(23 Maple Drive)

- Start with nine-point type as the smallest size on your cards if you are using Arial, Times New Roman or a similar-sized font. Lose the six- and seven-point sizes altogether.

- Choose a font style that is easy to read. Remember, different font types of the same point size look different. It has to do with the spacing of the letters. The following are all in nine-point type:

  Times New Roman Arial Century Gothic

- Use caution with trendy, light-colored type. It's more difficult to read.

- Keep in mind that most people with a color-vision deficiency have problems distinguishing between red and green.

TIPS: continued

- The most important element is your name. Put it in bold so it is easy to read, and make sure the font is well spaced. If it's not, the letters can blur together, making for difficult reading.

- Put the name you want to be called on your card. Utilize brackets if you use initials or a more formal name on your card. Examples: A.Y. (Tony) Johnson; Douglas (Doug).

- Make sure your cards work in a card scanner and capture all the information properly.

- Use your professional designation(s) if it is helpful for others to understand what you do and to establish your credentials.

- Use both sides of the card. The back is a good place to use color, place web site information, show the company slogan or list company awards.

- Leave some white space on your card.

- Use no more than two fonts (excluding logo).

- Make sure the type on the card is properly aligned with the margins.

- Keep information in logical blocks and use lines to separate the information.

- Use beige card stock with caution; sometimes it looks dull.

- When picking card stock, look at samples. A 110- lb. card stock in one brand may feel thinner than the same weight of stock in another brand. Err on the side of a stiffer stock, because flimsy paper can look cheap.

- Use caution when purchasing pre-printed designer card stock you can buy at an office supply store. Pick styles that look professional, and card stock that is not too flimsy.

- Consider a dye cut; a shape can make your card memorable.

- Avoid cards that can annoy, such as oversized, fold-over or laminated ones.

- If you don't understand design, layout and font type, get a professional to help you.

BIBLIOGRAPHY

Buchanan, Mark, *Nexus, Small Worlds and the Groundbreaking Science of Networks,* W.W. Norton & Company, Inc., 2002.

Dalai Lama XIV, *Live in a Better Way: Reflections on Truth, Love and Happiness,* Penguin Compass, 2002.

Gann, Ernest K, *A Hostage to Fortune,* Alfred A. Knopf, 1978.

Gladwell, Malcolm, *The Tipping Point: How Little Things Can Make a Big Difference,* Little Brown and Company, 2000.

Granovetter, Mark, "The Strength of Weak Ties," *American Journal of Sociology* 78, 1360-80, 1973.

Gross, Ronald, *Socrates' Way: Seven Master Keys to Using Your Mind to the Utmost,* J.P. Tarcher, 2002.

Hock, Dee, *Birth of the Chaordic Age,* Berrett-Koehler Publishers, Inc., 1999.

Hyde, Catherine Ryan, *Pay It Forward,* Pocket Books, 2000.

Legge, Peter, *Who Dares Wins,* Eaglet Publishing, 2001.

Newman, Peter C., *Titans,* The Penguin Group, 1998.

Proust, Marcel, *Remembrance of Things Past,* Knof, 1982.

Skousen, Mark, *Economic Logic,* Capital Press, 2002.

Watts, Duncan J. and Strogatz, Steven H., "Collective dynamics of 'small world' networks," *Nature* 393, 440-442, 1998.

Watts, Duncan J., *Small Worlds, The Dynamics of Networks between Order and Randomness,* Princeton Studies in Complexity, Princeton University Press, 1999.

Zander, Benjamin and Rosamund Stone, *The Art of Possibility,* Harvard Business School Press, 2000.

VISIT OUR POND

OUR NETWORK IS ALWAYS ON

Visit our pond at **www.frogandprince.com**

Order books for yourself, your friends and your employees.

Find out more about seminars, training sessions and speakers. All three of the authors are available to make presentations.

Frog and Prince Networking Corporation

Marrying the art and science of networking™

We want your small-worlds story.
Visit **www.frogandprince.com** to find out more.